THE

REIGN

OF THE LIONESSES

THE

REIGN
OF THE LIONESSES

How European Glory Changed
Women's Football in England

Carrie Dunn

First published by Pitch Publishing, 2023

Pitch Publishing
9 Donnington Park,
85 Birdham Road,
Chichester,
West Sussex,
PO20 7AJ
www.pitchpublishing.co.uk
info@pitchpublishing.co.uk

ISBN 978 180150636 6

Typesetting and origination by Pitch Publishing
Printed and bound in Great Britain by TJ Books Limited, Padstow

CONTENTS

DEDICATION

To my sister Philippa, who, if I'd asked her first, probably would have said she wanted me to write her a book solely about Lauren Hemp.

PROLOGUE

I HAVE never been the kind of sports fan who remembers statistics. Nor do I have the kind of memory that has instant recall of the entirety of a match. Instead, I remember the moments that have meant the very most to me, and the excitement, the happiness, that I felt.

So I know that in the years to come, when I think of the sunny, glorious days of July 2022, I'll remember it in a series of snapshots.

Assuring friends and colleagues after England's mediocre performance in the first match of the Women's Euros that it didn't matter, that the result was the only important thing, and the displays would follow.

The phone calls and incoming emails gradually ramping up as media outlets across the country and all over the world began to sense that this tournament was going to be something special for England; answering the phone at 6am and already primed to go on the radio and explain once again what a seminal summer this was proving to be.

Literally falling off my chair with the audacity of Alessia Russo's back-heel, the third of the Lionesses' goals against Sweden in the semi-final. I crashed on to the floor with a holler not of pain but of delight and incredulity.

Chloe Kelly scoring the winner in extra time of the final against Germany, checking mid-celebration that her moment of glory was not about to be stolen from her by the electronic eye of VAR.

The final whistle blowing, and me bursting into tears.

'Are you all right?' asked my husband – used to the intensity of my reactions when it comes to sport but having never seen me crying to such an extent.

I gathered myself enough to be able to reply through choking sobs: 'I'm just so HAPPY.'

The trite trilling about 'football coming home' was fun, of course. Initially a song laden with irony to mark the men's 1996 European Championships held in England, the chorus has taken on a life of its own. Fans wheel it out for their clubs and for their countries, a way to assert one's superiority and hopes for victory.

But it wasn't just about winning a trophy. It wasn't about seeing Beth Mead's beaming face on the front and back pages of every single newspaper I picked up, although the way these young women became superstars in the space of a month was truly thrilling.

Nor was it about the chatter in the pub and the corner shop being about the Lionesses, with everyone watching the matches, regardless of how casual their interest in football.

It wasn't even about those slightly smug memes on social media, noting that when an England senior team last won a major international tournament, back in 1966, women were still officially banned from playing the game at all – and wouldn't it be just so hilarious if they were the ones to 'bring it home' after all that time?

No. For me, it was about the women who had laid the groundwork, some of the most incredible women I have ever had the good fortune to get to know.

The women who set up their own leagues and competitions, found their own pitches, and got their own sponsorship deals, even when they weren't allowed to play on FA-affiliated grounds.

The so-called 'Lost Lionesses', who went to Mexico for an unofficial, unsanctioned Women's World Cup in 1971, suffered dire retribution, and never spoke about it – even to each other – for the next half-century.

The England squads who played for the honour of it and paid for their own travel, doing their own training and fitness work every night after work or school, using their holiday allowance so they could go to international tournaments and represent their country.

When the whistle blew – and after I calmed down – I picked up my phone, and emailed or texted dozens of these women. I congratulated them, because although Sarina Wiegman and her team lifted the trophy, the victory was one orchestrated in the decades before. Without the commitment and sacrifices of the previous generations, the triumphant, lauded Lionesses would never have been able to take to the Wembley turf at all.

Within a few minutes, my phone began to ping with responses. To a woman, they were thrilled to have seen such a triumph; some were there in the stadium, others were watching on television at home, but all of them felt as I did: that these forerunners of today's newly minted superstars had a share in the glory.

The phone calls and emails kept pouring in over the following few days. It was important, I thought, to set the Women's Euros victory in its context; yes, to remind people how long women had been banned from playing football in England, but also to remind them that winning one major international trophy was not and should never be the end of a story. These women – the elite of the elite – are full-time professional footballers, reaping the benefits of training every day with a ball at their feet, concentrating only on their skill, fitness and technique, just as their male counterparts have done for so many years.

But for each of those women clutching a gold medal, there are dozens more still struggling to make a living in the game, desperately trying to balance their home life with their playing career, facing the tough decision of whether to keep striving towards the aim of professional football or to play it safe and sensible by pursuing a steady career with a more stable income and a more secure future.

There are hundreds more further down the footballing pyramid who continue to fight to overcome the obstacles so entrenched in the game, with men's teams always taking precedence when it comes to funding and facilities, still dealing with people's tedious, lazy sexism.

And there are thousands of little girls who might want to lace up a pair of football boots – just like their brother, or their cousin, or their friend at school – but have always been told it's not a game for them, but for boys. If they haven't been dissuaded, they might seek out a team to join, and find that while there are scores of them for boys, they have to travel miles for a girls' club; while mixed football is still a possibility for youngsters, it is utterly understandable that teenage girls might prefer to be in a team with other teenage girls, simply to reduce their anxiety around trying a new sport. Or they may be looking ahead, thinking about progressing to the women's game in a year or two, and wanting to find a club that offers a clear pathway from junior to senior.

The Lionesses knew that perfectly well.

On Wednesday, 3 August – three days after they lifted their trophy at Wembley, two days after thousands of fans joined them in London's Trafalgar Square to celebrate – they released an open letter. In the midst of the governing Conservative Party's internal wrangling over who would win the vote to become the nation's next prime minister, the European champions called on the candidates to back women's football – for all age groups.

All 23 squad members put their names to a powerful call to action, saying: 'We want every young girl in the nation to be able to play football at school. Currently only 63 per cent of girls can play football in PE lessons. The reality is we are inspiring young girls to play football, only for many to end up going to school and not being able to play.'

That statistic came as a shock to many, but it was one quoted by the FA in the pre-tournament publicity as they set out their aim to get 75 per cent of girls playing football at school. The issue was not primary schools – where boys and girls tend to have the same sessions – but secondary schools, where boys and girls tend to be split by sex, and where female PE teachers may not have football as one of the sports they are most confident to coach.

The Lionesses had something to say about that, too.

'We ask you and your government to ensure that all girls have access to a minimum of two hours a week of PE,' they added. 'Not only should we be offering football to all girls, we also need to invest in and support female PE teachers too. Their role is crucial and we need to give them the resources to provide girls' football sessions. They are key role models from which so many young girls can flourish.'

The Lionesses acknowledged repeatedly over the course of the summer – and even before that – that they were role models for a generation of boys and girls. Over and over again, these players, young women in their twenties and thirties, talked about how they lacked female footballing role models when they were little.

Over and over again, I thought how lucky I had been to benefit from what I have come to think of as a strange mid-generational glitch. There remains little tangible evidence of it, but in the late 1980s and early 1990s, Channel 4 showed women's football matches – both live and highlights. It was there that I first became aware of the all-conquering Doncaster Belles, for example, and there that I first saw players of the calibre of Karen Walker, Gill Coultard, Marieanne Spacey and more. For just a few years – as far as I can ascertain now, the years before the FA finally took the women's game in house and in hand – I, as a little girl, could watch women playing football on one of the four television channels we had available to watch back then. The little girls who love football now, of course, have it even better: domestic league and cup fixtures as well as international clashes available on terrestrial television, streaming and cable. They live in a world where the England team who finally brought football home is female.

SUMMER

1

Retention

ELLEN WHITE, born in 1989, would have been too young to remember Channel 4 showing women's football. Early in her career, she had talked about her parents and her brother being her role models when she was small. Indeed, it was her father who set her on the road to footballing stardom, signing her up to the 'Mini Ducks' kids' programme he ran in their home town of Aylesbury. In terms of players who inspired her, though, she often mentioned two England legends, both men: Gary Lineker, for the sheer number of goals he scored, and David Beckham, for his professionalism on and off the field.

For many of the female players of White's generation, the first real awareness they had of the possibility of playing professional football was watching the movie *Bend It Like Beckham*, released in 2002. Even then, the plot focused on the very best female talent having the opportunity to move to America and pursue a footballing career there; there was still no chance of it happening in England.

White visited the USA as a child, and had the opportunity to meet England star Kelly Smith, then playing for Philadelphia Charge. That was the first genuine realisation she had that she – a girl living in an English town – could play elite football and represent her country. White and Smith later became team-mates for club and country; and it was Smith who set the England goalscoring record that White later claimed.

Having her face plastered all over the front page of a newspaper, though, was something White was used to at an early age. As a nine-year-old in September 1998, she discovered that she was no longer allowed to play alongside boys in their local league, the Chiltern Youth League. The local newspaper, the *Bucks Herald*, covered the story with the headline 'Soccer girl banned by league for boys', and reported that she had scored over 100 goals in the season before. FA rules, the newspaper declared, allowed for mixed football up to and including the age of ten, but the local league said that girls were not allowed in what they saw as a boys-only competition. The photos of White accompanying the news story were of her in full Arsenal kit; she was already captaining their under-11 side.

Twenty-four years later, White announced her retirement from football as a newly crowned European champion. After 113 international caps and 52 goals, plus two Women's Super League titles, three Women's FA Cups and countless more honours, she had concluded that all her dreams had come true on 31 July.

'This has been one of the hardest decisions of my life but one that I know is the right decision for me,' she wrote in a statement she released on social media. 'This decision has always been one I have wanted to make on my terms.

And this is my time to say goodbye to football and watch the next generation shine. It has been my greatest honour and privilege to play this game. In particular playing for England has and always will be the greatest gift.'

Stepping back from international football after winning the biggest prize of her career was perhaps something observers expected from the 33-year-old; retiring from club football was more of a shock. A few days later, she revealed that her decision had been hastened by suffering a punctured lung in 2021, when she was receiving acupuncture for her long-standing back problem. Remarkably, she had recovered, returned to full fitness, and got back into the England squad without a word of it leaking to the press. She told the media that she had gone into the Euros knowing full well that it was her last hurrah, and that she would be announcing her retirement afterwards.

'It was a lot for me to have to go through and a big reason that accelerated my want to retire,' she told the BBC a few days afterwards.

The next major retirement was even more of a surprise, in a way. Jill Scott – two years White's senior – had been utterly dedicated to her England career. Finding herself out of the Manchester City first team, she opted to spend time out on loan at Everton and then Aston Villa, ensuring she was match fit and available for selection for both the 2021 Olympic Games and then the Euros. Her presence was the tangible thread connecting the current generation with the previous ones; she had played in the 2007 Women's World Cup, when her 2022 Lionesses squad-mate Hannah Hampton, 14 years her junior, was still in primary school.

She finished her career as England's second-most-capped player – and announced her departure in a way that truly suited her personality, in a first-person essay published on The Players' Tribune website that completely captured her voice and style of speech. She reiterated throughout that she had promised herself that she would not cry when she finally bade football farewell, but the reaction from readers indicated that plenty of them shed more than a few tears reading her emotional love letter to the game that gave her so much. She admitted that when she was called into Sarina Wiegman's office to find out whether or not she had made the 2022 squad, she was shaking, explaining: 'I knew it was my last go. I just wanted to give absolutely everything I had left to this team, no matter what that meant.'

Scott did not start any of England's matches during the Euros, but she remained a crucial part of the squad. She came on as a substitute in the second group game, for the last ten minutes; in the quarter-final, for the last four minutes of extra time; in the semi-final, for the last four minutes of the match; and in the final, in the last minute of normal time. Altogether it might have totalled only a handful of minutes, but they were crucial ones; under pressure, with the Lionesses needing to hold on to a result, it was Scott who was called on, ever reliable, able to adapt and hold her nerve. Her departure truly marked the end of an era.

* * *

More than a decade since the launch of the Women's Super League, one of their aims was starting to look just a little bit wobbly. They had intended to make the league the most attractive domestic competition in the world, retaining English talent. It was a step meant to prevent a brain-drain that had become all too common in the women's game, with players stepping up to the senior set-up and then immediately heading over to the USA, where they were able to gain a college education as well as play football at a very high level. Some of the younger Lionesses had taken that route: Lotte Wubben-Moy and Alessia Russo both played for the North Carolina Tar Heels, for example.

But as leagues around Europe began to raise their game – wanting more competition to improve their Women's Champions League performances and in turn their national team – they also became more and more alluring. Of course, with England players now elevated to bona fide superstardom, the giants of European football were interested in adding them to their squads, and perhaps this was not just for their skill on the pitch but for their name value and the opportunities for off-field branding and merchandising they would bring. Georgia Stanway headed to Bayern Munich, Lucy Bronze and Keira Walsh both to Barcelona.

The Spanish league had been particularly notable for its development in recent years as the big hitters of the men's game started to plough money into the women's teams. Barcelona had already won the Women's Champions League in 2020/21, and were collating a team of international superstars – not just Bronze and Walsh but Norway's Ingrid Engen and Caroline Graham Hansen and Nigeria's Asisat Oshoala, for example, as well as Spanish talent such as Sandra Panos, Mapi Leon and the much-celebrated Alexia

Putellas, Ballon d'Or winner and FIFA's Best Female Player of 2021.

They were also bringing fans into the stands. In 2021/22, they faced Real Madrid in the quarter-finals of the Champions League, with 91,552 fans at the home leg, the second match of the tie, and then Wolfsburg in the semi-final, watched by 91,648 in the first leg at Camp Nou. Inevitably, these figures caused a great deal of excitement, with many asserting that these were the biggest-ever attendances for any women's football match; this was likely a well-intentioned exaggeration due to a lack of awareness about the unofficial Women's World Cup in 1971, where matches packed out the Azteca Stadium in Mexico, with a capacity of around 110,000 at that point.

The Lionesses could certainly command audiences of that size, if such stadia were available to them, but in the Women's Super League matters were on a somewhat smaller scale. WSL teams continued, in the main, to play at smaller grounds, with the occasional 'big match' at their parent men's ground; Manchester United Women, who usually played their home matches at Leigh Sports Village, had already announced that they would be playing Aston Villa at Old Trafford in December, when the men's season was on hiatus due to the scheduling of the winter World Cup in Qatar; Liverpool were permitted to play at Anfield when they were due to host Everton in the last weekend of September.

That was also the weekend when Arsenal would be playing at the Emirates Stadium against their north London rivals Tottenham Hotspur. At the start of September, the match already looked likely to break all WSL attendance records. Gunners manager Jonas Eidevall, however, was adamant that playing in the Emirates Stadium was not a stunt, but a viable step forward for women's football – something that could happen more regularly, and was something that the customer base was demanding, not just a fun gimmick to attract casually interested passers-by, wanting to be part of an exciting occasion. At the same time, he was very careful to highlight the Gunners' track record as a pioneer club for the women's game, paying tribute to the work done by coaches and players of previous generations.

'Remember it's 50,000 sold tickets,' Eidevall said to the media, emphasising the commercial benefit of putting a women's match in a bigger stadium – more tickets could be sold, meaning more income generated for the club. 'It's not giveaways, it's not sold for a discounted price; it's sold tickets. I think that's really, really special because that means doing this, the way the club has done it, it's sustainable. It shows that the interest there is for real.

'The investment that we as a team, the club has done, but also the past generations, the teams before us have done to put us on to this stage here, that's phenomenal. We feel that, and of course we want to go out, and we want to make the most of it so it can happen again more frequently.'

Intriguingly, Eidevall cast his eyes wider. He pointed out to the press that the clubs in the top echelons of European football were those who were part of big set-ups led by successful men's clubs; he reminded them that when Arsenal won what is now the Women's Champions League, independent clubs for women, such as Sweden's Umea or Germany's Turbine Potsdam, were competing for the crown.

'Today, when you look at the clubs going into the quarter-finals of the Champions League, there are no women's-only clubs left,' he said. 'They are all clubs who have top teams in men's football.

'But what you have to see there is that there is only one consistent member and that's Arsenal. That's class and that's history and that is something that you can never change. You were a first mover, you were a believer before everyone else.

'That is something the club and all the fans should be very, very proud of.'

It was an interesting observation. Many football governing bodies around the world have in recent years encouraged their men's clubs – particularly at the top end of the game – to take women's football within their remit, and provide financial support as well as infrastructure. The idea is that a long-established men's club acts almost as a guarantor for the women's team, still essentially in its infancy after so many years of the game's growth being deliberately stunted or ignored. The prize money in men's football is greater than that on offer to women, by some degree; of course, the salaries on offer in the men's game are also much greater than those in the women's game, as are the advertising endorsements. Women's football is only now beginning to understand the true commercial power it might hold.

For the 2022/23 season, the FA and lead sponsor Vitality announced an impressive increase to the Women's FA Cup prize fund. From a pot swelled to £3 million, a club who lost in the first round of qualifying would still pick up £450, with a team losing in the first round proper getting a little solace with £1,500, and the eventual winners earning £100,000. Such sums might, of course, raise an eyebrow within the men's game, where the money on offer in 2022/23 for the two finalists in the Emirates FA Cup alone totalled £3 million, but it would be worth remembering that just the season before, the women's cup winners collected just £25,000.

The inequalities between the men's and women's sides of the game have often been a topic of conversation among fans and pundits. Some might argue that explicit comparisons of the two are not entirely helpful; with women's football essentially banned up until the 1970s, and with even more social and cultural barriers to break after the explicit prohibition was lifted, there remains much work to be done to give the women's game the soundest of structures at all levels, just as the men have.

As the clock ticked down to the start of the women's domestic season, a familiar rumour began to circulate – that the Premier League, the operators of the men's top tier of professional football, were interested in taking over the Women's Super League as well.

The Premier League's chief executive Richard Masters confirmed to journalists that they were 'in active conversations' about how they could help the women's and girls' game more, in addition to their new offer of funding to the tune of £21 million, split between grassroots and professional football. He avoided any discussion of an outright WSL takeover but it had been raised many times previously – most notably and most recently by the former Arsenal striker Ian Wright, now a regular TV pundit for women's matches, who had mentioned it after the Lionesses' Euro triumph.

Indeed, Masters himself had broached the possibility two summers previously, when he told the parliamentary select committee for digital culture, media and sport that he would like to see it happen.

He – and others in the men's game – may have been surprised by the lack of enthusiasm his remarks engendered among those in the women's game, which could explain his more circumspect approach in 2022. There had been a great deal of disquiet among those at WSL clubs, concerned that they would find themselves facing some big problems if the Premier League were in charge. With women's professional football in England still in its relative infancy, there were concerns that its sustainability had yet to be guaranteed; coach and player development for women is still relatively new, with many young players still pursuing tertiary education in a way that their male peers do not. Some within the women's game worried that if the Premier League took over, they would simply roll out their existing structures without taking the time and effort to invest in the unique needs and challenges that were still in existence.

Other observers were concerned that a Premier League takeover would ultimately lead to the top two tiers of women's football simply reflecting the men's game. By 2022, the WSL had what was colloquially referred to as a 'Big Four' – Arsenal, Chelsea, Manchester City and Manchester United – the quartet are all, of course, linked to massive and financially rich men's clubs. However, at the start of the WSL, when the geographical spread of teams was an important criterion, as was a spread of talent to ensure competition, the league also included Doncaster Rovers Belles, Bristol Academy and Lincoln (later Notts County, who folded in 2017 a few days before the start of the Spring Series competition). The loss of so-called smaller clubs from the top tier was perhaps inevitable in the push towards professionalisation, with only the biggest and richest clubs able to afford the wages and facilities.

However, the Championship – the second tier – continued to boast some names that would not be familiar to an onlooker who followed only the men's game: for example, Coventry United, Durham Women, and Lewes. The semi-professional status of the league meant that independent women's teams or those less well-off or those with a different structure to the traditional football club were all able to thrive, competing against the typically big names so well known from their exploits in the men's game.

Lewes, in Sussex, had grabbed plenty of press attention for their commitment to equal pay for their men's and women's teams. Certain elements of the media have been fond of trying to stir up controversy by asking female players if they thought they deserved the same salaries as their male counterparts; Lewes's decision, made publicly, eliminated such questions from the discussion around their squad, at least. Their pay equality might have been an eye-catching policy, but as their CEO Maggie Murphy explained, it was simply a manifestation of the way in which they were building a new, different style of football club. They were preparing to hold elections to the club's board, with three vacancies to serve for three years – an unusual way for a football club to govern itself.

'People always want to jump to the money straight away,' said Murphy, 'and what I try to say is that it's actually really about equal decision-making, and everything else falls in with trying to build an ethical, community-oriented, transparent, well-governed football club. When you try to do that, then equality follows suit, and that's why we split our pay equally, because we think it's the right thing to do for our community and for the world.'

2

Anchor

SCANNING DOWN the names of the clubs in the women's football pyramid, your eye might be drawn to one particularly poetic one in the fourth tier. It is not a name that has decades of history attached to it; nor is it a name shared with a men's team.

London Seaward adopted their name in 2021, and are happy to explain the thought process behind its creation.

'Our club's history is indelibly linked to our home, and our future is as well,' reads their website. 'And that home is a city of rivers. A maritime city. A city built on the hopes and dreams offered by the sea.'

Based in east London, their independence is emblazoned across their digital footprint, and is an intrinsic part of their ethos.

But London Seaward were the spiritual successors of another team who had enjoyed a close link with a men's club for six years.

Leyton Orient Women had taken on the east London men's club's name, colours and badge as they rose up the women's football pyramid, and enjoyed considerable success, becoming an established part of the fourth tier FA Women's National League Division One South-East.

Danni Griffiths had worn the captain's armband for Orient with pride. She had acknowledged for several years that she was coming to the end of her playing career, wondering if she would hang up her boots if and when she had children. External events, however, forced her hand, ultimately making her decision for her.

It began with the 2019/20 season, which she already knew would be an interrupted one for her; she and her wife, who married in May 2019, were heading off on honeymoon at the end of the year.

'We agreed with our respective works that we could have two months off over the Christmas period,' she recalled. 'I discussed with Chris [Brayford, then-Orient Women's manager] the extent of my involvement [with the squad], because I was very conscious that [being away] would be disruptive for the team. He wanted me to continue as captain but I said, "I want someone to be a designated vice-captain if that is the case because I don't feel right leaving in the middle of the season so I want some continuity for everyone."'

Sophie Le Marchand was appointed vice-captain and took the armband when Griffiths was away. It was a season of change for Orient regardless; the spine of the team, who had picked up so much silverware in the years before, was ageing together, necessitating an influx of new, younger players.

'The start of that season was a mixed bag,' said Griffiths. 'It took a while for us all to gel. We had a core of the team but we had a lot of good new players that joined, but working out how we all fit together – it wasn't as easy as we would have probably hoped.'

With Orient out of the Women's FA Cup by the middle of December but rolling along in mid-table in the league, Griffiths flew off to the other side of the globe to enjoy her honeymoon, but the newly-weds began to notice that it did not feel like the usual experience of travel. Visiting South East Asia and heading over to Australasia, they saw their fellow travellers beginning to use facemasks more and more regularly as news began to circulate about a new form of coronavirus that was spreading rapidly.

Griffiths and her wife returned to England at the start of February with the Covid-19 pandemic beginning to take hold. It had a swift impact on football, of course. After Orient's trip to AFC Basildon on 8 March, all their subsequent fixtures for that season were cancelled, and ultimately in June the season was declared null and void, with all the results for the National League Division One South-East wiped from the record books. The curtailment of that season also marked the end of Griffiths' playing career; it was not the way she would have expected, but it was necessary.

'It was around that time that we were thinking about moving out of London anyway, and Covid fast-tracked that decision,' she said. 'We wanted a bit more space – working on the dining room table wasn't the most productive way to be doing things. It was going to be more difficult to get to training, get to games, which was already difficult with a full-time job.'

There was another factor that swayed Griffiths; she and her wife had decided the time had come to start a family.

They had always agreed that when they made that decision, it would mean the end of playing football regularly. That long-term planning meant there was no real argument over it, but it did not make it easier for Griffiths to accept in practice.

'I always knew that when family came around that it would take priority, and I didn't have much spare time when I was playing and working, so to make time, something had to give,' she said. Speaking with the benefit of two years' distance from her official retirement, Griffiths acknowledged that she was sad about it at the time, but the unusual circumstances that ended that final season also did her a favour.

'[Without the pandemic], I wouldn't have known when that end point would have come,' she said. 'I was always going to keep playing as long as I was playing with the girls that I was playing with at the time, and I was enjoying it.

'I'm more breezy about it now and Covid has relaxed me a bit more. It would have been a more difficult decision had it not been for that.'

Griffiths and her wife became proud parents to a daughter in the last days of 2021. Being a mother with a busy career as a lawyer meant no time to dwell on what might have been when it came to football.

'It's actually nice having a two-day weekend – I don't think I've had a two-day weekend since I was 10 or 11, I've always played sport!' she smiled. 'But I do miss [playing] to an extent. I miss the social side, and the exercise – it's much more difficult to exercise as a parent.

'I played in a men's five-a-side tournament recently, and I scored some goals, which was surprising as a defender. I joked with my wife the other day because I saw an advert for our local team – their ladies' team was looking for some people to go down to training and play games, and I said, "Well, I won't play the games on Sunday, but I could go down to training?" She was like, "I thought you were giving up!" The temptation is always there!'

However, she felt a kinship with London Seaward, despite never representing them under their current banner.

'When I was involved in the club, I did go to the meetings with the directors and senior leadership of the Leyton Orient club as a whole,' she said, recalling the discussions around funding to enable the women's team to continue at their high level. 'They were difficult conversations. I understand both points of view. We wanted to continue growing as a women's club, and they had their own targets for the men and on the business as a whole.'

In 2021, the team formerly known as Leyton Orient Women finally sheared off, and began their new life as London Seaward.

'I felt the frustration and the hurt that the girls were feeling, particularly girls I still knew, but also people that had joined the club, because we had worked hard to try and build that relationship and to represent them for a number of years and we had some good success. I felt for everyone involved.'

She added: 'We were a club before Leyton Orient, and they are still a club after Leyton Orient – same principles. Hopefully they'll have good success as their new brand.'

* * *

Jo Butler-Williams, one of Seaward's players, had been there throughout the at-times complicated and painful handover from Orient to Seaward.

She had joined the club in June 2021, just as the switchover was happening, and noticed the amount of tiredness and frustration within the set-up as they struggled to solve problems from pitch access to player signings. Long-time Orient manager Brayford stepped down from his role in the autumn, with another member of the coaching staff taking a job offer in the Women's Championship. Seaward were sinking.

Butler-Williams plus some team-mates pulled together a working group to run things – and their first task was to ensure that they had someone to take charge of team matters. Dan McKimm, who had been coaching with the club, was someone Butler-Williams had known for a long time, stemming back to their time at university in Birmingham. She asked him to stay at the club and head up the team in what would prove to be a challenging season.

'Financially we needed to do a lot of work to get us to survive the year so there was a lot of work that went into that,' reflected Butler-Williams. 'Four teams were being relegated from our league – our closest geographical teams all went down, and these teams all had some significant backing behind them as well, so last season became a bit of a "just keep the cogs turning", "try and get anything to work", and we ended up doing a lot better than we expected – sixth in the table. It's not brilliant, but it's not bad.'

The 2022/23 season had, however, started much more brightly, with an agreement to ground-share in Waltham

Forest, and the Seaward reserves also playing there, creating more of a unified club philosophy. They became a company limited by guarantee, and also put a full committee in place, with each person taking on an area of responsibility. Christine Dunning, mother of player Rebecca, stepped in as chair. Her daughter had played in the second and third tiers before, but was looking for an opportunity to enjoy her football alongside building her off-pitch career.

'She went along to Seaward and was very impressed with the vision and direction of travel and actually the players – she felt they were very much an inclusive bunch, she felt very comfortable with them,' said Dunning. 'And she came home and said, "I think I'm going to sign for these guys." She had options, she had actually been offered pay to play as well, and she was saying, "It's not about the money but how it feels."'

Not long after that, and now a Seaward player, Rebecca mentioned that the club needed a chairperson and thought her mother – a former company director – would be good at the job. Dunning was slightly reticent, with plenty of other time commitments as a magistrate, but on enquiry, Butler-Williams assured her it would only take up two hours a week. She decided to put herself forward, feeling it was important that she did so.

'I've got another daughter who's 18 and she also plays football,' she explained. 'I've got a son and he doesn't play football because his sisters are too good at it, so he plays rugby! It's been contagious, with the Women's Euros, hearing the challenges that women's teams have faced, hearing about teams folding, underfunding – I felt like I could probably bring my skills to help.'

Dunning's time commitment to her job as football club chair is not, however, limited to two hours per week, despite Butler-Williams's best efforts at an accurate estimate.

'The joys of a growing organisation is there's always something else to add to the to-do list!' Butler-Williams smiled. 'Last year was more about survival, and therefore I didn't quite equate it – we have more possibilities, there's more endless possibilities. Before, it was about "we can create a club that ticks over and is sustained", whereas now we really have got a serious team on a foundation that people are throwing in a new idea or a new concept or a thought.

'The two hours, although that maybe was on the smaller side, it's because we're trying to achieve more and because we have ambitions. We are really seeing as an organisation everybody is now getting used to their roles and getting used to what the protocol is, what's the process, when do we do it, how do we do it, so I think as we get better and better, Christine's role gets smaller and smaller.'

One of the most important factors they had to consider was funding. They were not being subsidised by a wealthy men's club, nor did they have a benefactor bankrolling them. They did, however, have one lead sponsor – a technical writing firm based in the USA, who stumped up some money to enable them to operate for the season.

'We are outperforming our backing that we have, quite substantially,' pointed out Butler-Williams. 'The reason we've always outperformed is because it's about an environment. We don't just recruit players based on their football ability. It's about fitting with being inclusive and caring and supportive.'

That was particularly important to Butler-Williams. She had previously played at a club where she hated going to training sessions and would cry on her way home, and she liked that Seaward attracted talent not because they offered huge sums of money, but because it was a nice place to play football. Dunning, as chair, acknowledged that having wages on offer was starting to shape the women's game even at their level.

'The women's game is changing,' she said. 'We recognise that ultimately if they were playing at this level in the men's game, they would be being paid, no question, so it's something that we are having to consider: how are we going to get to that point, because our competitors are going to do it? At the moment [players at other clubs] might get a couple of hundred pounds a month or something, so that's not too much of a draw, but when it becomes a bit more than that, it is going to turn people's heads. I don't think a few hundred pounds will, but I think a few thousand will, and we are thinking, "How are we going to compete?" Because although we make people feel warm and fuzzy, that may not be enough when there's more money on the table.'

'Especially because we want to be a club that's inclusive – then not paying people could almost become a reason that you can't play here,' added Butler-Williams. 'We are absolutely trying to build that infrastructure but it's interesting, the disparities within the women's game. You have clubs that are paying every player at our level versus clubs that aren't paying anybody and can't even field a team of 11. It's just insane, the level of differences in there at the minute. Even clubs two or three tiers below [Seaward] are still paying players.'

Independence offered Seaward plenty of opportunity, certainly, but it also tied their hands in many ways. It required creative thinking from the club's committee, and absolute buy-in from players and the backroom staff.

'We're keen to exploit the areas that we can,' said Butler-Williams, pointing to the merchandise they were able to sell. 'We can sell a kit. Most women's sides that are tied to men's sides have to go through procedures: who gets the money, where does it go from, how does it come? There's all of that complication behind the decision-making. That's where we want to make sure that we can push as quick as possible, to build that behind us.'

Replica kit, however, is an item bought by fans, and London Seaward recognised that if they could attract people through the turnstile, who would then spend money in the ground, their lives would be much easier.

'Really, our income is driven by who comes through the gate and we've got targets around that,' said Dunning. The club were thankful for the increased Women's FA Cup prize money, meaning even a brief run in the competition would bring a financial reward. In the meantime, London Seaward continued to seek further sponsorship, with players making contributions if they were not able to secure their own personal sponsor.

'It's expensive to train twice a week,' added Dunning. 'It's expensive to have two teams that you've got to provide pitches and referees for. It's an issue for the women's game if you want to be an independent team. We've got to be very creative, and desirable.'

* * *

London Seaward got their lead sponsor, TechSoc, through a series of Twitter threads that went viral in the wake of England's win at the 2022 Women's Euros. It highlighted the inequalities that still riddle football, discussing issues including pitch access for training and matches, and why kit designed and created for female footballers is so important. Those tweets were spotted by Curtis Frye, a writer in Portland, Oregon, who noticed that Seaward were also seeking finance to enable them to counter some of these obstacles they were facing.

'I asked if they were open to Americans,' Frye grinned. 'They said "Sure", and there you go.'

Frye and his wife Ginny already had a tenuous connection with the Waltham Forest area, having visited the William Morris Gallery on a previous visit to London. However, he was more drawn by the story of an independent football club for women, who wanted support to survive and had been struggling on by themselves for a year at that point.

'They wouldn't have done that [season of struggle] if it [wasn't] worth something to them,' he said, 'and so I thought that I could jump in and offer support. I have no doubt that they would have found a way to survive without me, but this type of sponsorship makes life a lot easier.'

'He is an absolute gem,' Jo Butler-Williams had enthused earlier. 'I've had a lot of challenging conversations across the last year and I thought within seconds [of talking to Frye], "You're just a great egg." He was talking about wealth redistribution: "I've had a lot of privilege, and I just want to support you, and I want to take the pressure off and give you an environment that you can challenge and strive in terms of not feeling the pressure financially, to compensate here and there." He's an incredible sponsor and hopefully we can carry on that relationship into next season and beyond.'

Frye did not consider himself a fervent football fan, but living in Portland, he followed the fortunes of their men's team, the Timbers, and the women, the Thorns. With both teams well established and successful, local sponsorship opportunities were limited.

'I thought this would be an interesting way to step out of my writer shell,' he said. 'As a writer, I tend to be fairly solitary, and also because I work with technology, I don't have to interview people and form a narrative. For football, you're looking at individuals and a club organised to play at a high level. What I saw was football being played at a serious level by people who are serious about the game and who continued against significant odds to stay at tier four and avoid relegation.'

His new connection with London Seaward gave him additional reason to return to England; he had an itinerary for November that would enable him to explore the Waltham Forest area further, watch the team play, but also pop up to Manchester to see Sir Matthew Bourne's *Sleeping Beauty* ballet, and to enjoy some improvisational comedy with Comedy Sports Manchester – a group with whom he had previously performed.

'I have a short attention span and a good memory,' he joked when pressed about his variety of interests. 'I want all the knowledge, I want all the degrees, I want to read every book. Part of what I need to do as a supporter is to hold back, because Seaward don't need my advice about how to run a football club and certainly not about how to play football. So [all I have to do is] give them support, cheer them on, and if they have a question, answer it – other than that, my opinions would probably not be helpful!'

* * *

What Frye could offer was more than enough, and evidently incredibly appreciated. Dan McKimm, the Seaward first-team coach, was well aware that the financial resources on offer did not compare with plenty of their rivals in terms of numbers, but how the money was used created a competitive, attractive environment.

'We've got loads more [resources] this year than we did last year,' he acknowledged. 'When I took over at the time I did, I remember we got through that first game at Actonians, and then on the Monday, it was a case of trying to sit down and unpack where the club was actually at.

'There were a lot of challenges around actually trying to make the club viable and sustainable, and I remember at one point being in a case where we were like, "We've got six weeks to go until Christmas; we've just got to try and survive till that point." So coming from a place where you're in that situation to now, where we're stable, the best we can be at the moment, it's a world of difference, so already there's been massive progress in that side of things.

'The likes of Curt coming on board and his sponsorship, just from a hard cash perspective is massive as well, but also the pull that you feel, the validation around the club – you've got people there in your corner, and fighting for you, and people that care about building this project up. That's massive. I'm pretty confident we've still got the smallest budget in the league. We've got a much smaller budget than most of the teams in the league below as well – that's the hand you're dealt. As a coach, I can't do anything about that. My job is to create an environment that is attractive for people to want to come and play in. It's to prepare players, the team, to go out every Sunday and to be able to realise their potential on that particular day.'

McKimm began playing football himself as a child, representing the Bristol Rovers Academy for a spell, and started coaching as a young teenager, helping out some friends who ran some after-school football clubs. When he went to university in Birmingham, they agreed to pay for his Level 2 coaching qualification in return for him giving his time back to coach in the community as a volunteer. He spent some time coaching in primary schools before getting a spot with the university's women's football club. It was a big chance for him – not just in terms of practicalities, enabling him to coach on the university campus rather than having to travel across the city, but also a step into a world he knew little about. He had never coached women before, and now, as an 18-year-old, he was about to coach some high-profile and highly talented players.

'I remember walking down to the first session – I was super nervous,' he recalled. 'They had some really big-name players at the university: Izzy Christiansen who's now Everton captain, an England player, she was there; Laura Cooper, who at the time was with the England under-21s and Aston Villa; and a couple of others that were playing for big clubs.'

McKimm learnt plenty under programme manager Jenny Sugarman – who went on to coach at Villa and later to manage West Brom – and stayed with the women's club, establishing a third team and creating a development pathway during his time at university. After he graduated, he coached Coventry United's reserve side, and then moved to London in 2020, where he started working with Leyton Orient. When the women split from the men's club and became Seaward, McKimm was working within the coaching team that was already in place and they did not expect too much to change.

'There are two things that unite a group: extreme success and extreme adversity, and we faced the latter,' he said. 'The group was actually really, really strong. Leyton Orient can take their name away, they can take their brand away, but really in the cold light of day the football club wasn't their name – the football club is the people that made the club what it was, and that still all existed.

'We lost a couple [of players] because in times of uncertainty like that, there's always going to be nervousness. We're playing at that level where people want to progress and they're trying to make careers out of it and we always had decent players, there were always clubs sniffing around for our players. But the core of the group stayed. Having the players to put on the pitch was less of an issue; more of the issue was do we have a kit for them to play in? Do we have a name to play in? Do we have a ground to play at? The logistics of it was the real challenge.'

A few weeks into the season, when two of the coaching team departed for different reasons, the pressure was on McKimm to step up.

'It all unravelled on a Saturday,' he recalled, remembering a phone call from one of the board telling him that then-head coach Chris Brayford was stepping down while another coach had joined another team in a higher division. 'It was lots of different moving parts. We were in some trouble at that point. I was at football myself, playing on Saturday, and yeah it was like, "Wow, OK, tomorrow we've got to turn up and play a game against a team in the league," and it's the kind of game we needed to make sure we were getting points from, so it was quite a big ask. I hadn't really had any time with the players on the training pitch. I hadn't been around loads at the start of the season due to a couple of things that were going on, so yeah, it was tough. It was Saturday night, and then we rolled up on the Sunday at home and we got a really good draw against what turned out to be one of the better teams in the league that year.'

With McKimm in post, he now had the prerogative of shaping his squad while buying into the Seaward guiding principles. Of course, this was all in addition to his day job in IT recruitment, a line of work that did not guarantee regular office hours. He drew on his contacts as well as the existing club volunteers to put together an infrastructure that enabled players to play a competitive level of football but also receive the care and support they required. He knew that it was possible that this might give the players a platform to showcase themselves and move up to play for a higher-ranked club, but equally he knew that the set-up would continue to attract more good prospects.

'One thing I've tried to do since that first day in charge is create an environment that is as professional as it can be through what we can offer in services,' he said. 'The two things that we are trying to sell the club on is firstly the group, the players. In the ten years I've been involved in the women's game, I've never worked with a group that has such a strong culture as this group does. There's no ego, no bitchiness. They are a fantastic group of humans as well as fantastic players, and I think that's massive, especially at this level; you get a lot of ego, you get a lot of self-interest and stuff like that which can be a real poison to club culture. We have worked really hard to create a culture that's the complete opposite and antidote of that. It's actually really rare to find a genuine environment like that.'

The second big selling point was the set-up. Without wages on offer, McKimm was glad to be able to offer a nutrition specialist, a highly-qualified strength and conditioning coach, plus a physiotherapy team who were almost always available for appointments.

'When we have new players coming in, we are always hearing it's so much more professionally run and organised than places that people have been before,' he said. 'We pride ourselves on that because some teams and some clubs have the luxury of being able to wave cash at people, which speaks. We are not, so we have to try and create an environment that's so much better than everyone else's so that players want to come and play here and want to develop their careers with us.'

AUTUMN

3

Legend

A PRESS release from the FA hit journalists' inboxes in September, announcing that the forthcoming friendly international between European champions England and world champions the USA would be dedicated to marking the 50th anniversary of the official England women's team.

Over 100 former internationals were invited to Wembley as part of the celebrations, with the 1972 squad taking a central role. Two hundred and twenty-seven women had, at that point, been capped at senior level by England, and the FA were now awarding each of them their own 'legacy number', unique to them, showing their position in the team's history – from first-ever goalkeeper Sue Buckett with the number 1.

On the evening of Friday, 18 November, the first-ever Lionesses were welcomed to the national stadium, and much to their surprise they were finally awarded the formal England caps they had never received during their playing careers along with a shirt emblazoned with their name. When the Women's FA ran the international team, volunteer Flo Bilton hand-stitched each player a single souvenir cap; a much-treasured memento, but not the same as the plush velvet handed out to every man who had represented his country.

Sue Whyatt had been in the first ever official England squad in 1972, at the age of 15, although she did not make the starting XI for the inaugural match. Neither she nor any of her team-mates had been expecting any special ceremony for them at Wembley; as far as they knew, they would simply walk around the pitch at half-time, as they had done previously. On a tour of the stadium ahead of the match, though, they found that their route took them into the home changing room.

'We got to the England dressing room, [and I thought,] "Hang on, why are we coming this way?" And all of a sudden we were taken into that dressing room, and there's all these caps on a table, and our shirts hanging in those spaces for the players. Yeah, well – I filled up. I had tears rolling down my face. We were just open-mouthed.'

Current England captain Leah Williamson and the recently retired veteran Jill Scott led the presentation to the 1972 squad. It was a quiet, private, personal moment of celebration of and for these trailblazers ahead of their lap of honour in front of a capacity crowd later that evening. Whyatt concluded that even though it had taken half a century for the formal recognition from the FA, she did not mind the wait. She knew that it took the Lionesses' triumph on the international stage to finally force the decision-makers' hands, and that any recognition any earlier would have been low key, low profile, and would have failed to bring the 1972 squad's stories to a wider audience. For

Whyatt, at the age of 65, she felt she was at just the right point in her life to truly enjoy a little bit of celebrity, filming videos for social media with current England goalkeeper Mary Earps, and guesting on radio and television shows.

'I've always been quite – I wouldn't say "confident", but happy to say my own things. I don't usually mince my words,' she said. 'It's been good to have a voice and be able to just tell the story. It's been great to go on TV. I know I swore on *Woman's Hour* – "just give us our bloody caps!" – but that's how I felt. I have said that the FA have been really bad, but they have made up for it, and I said that as well – they have done their best, so this is a whole different FA now from those old fuddy-duddies who stopped [women from playing football]. You can't blame the ones that are in charge now for what happened in the past.'

Still, she was painfully aware that she was only getting these opportunities now because Sue Buckett, who played in goal in the very first international, was not in a position to take them on.

'I feel like I'm riding on Sue's tails, really, because she's not been able to do things,' Whyatt reflected. 'Obviously they're going to ask her first because she was number 1, and that's right, but because she's not feeling that she can do things, I'm getting all that reflected glory, really. I feel very conflicted about it a lot of the time, but I know we've still got to get the story out there.

'So many people don't know anything about it at all. I went and did a talk in a school the other day and they had no idea about the ban, not a clue. I ended up talking to the footballers afterwards, the boys and the girls, and I got some really nice feedback off the parents, saying how the kids had gone back absolutely full of the story.'

One of the 1972 team-mates Whyatt had stayed in touch with over the years was midfielder Janet Clark, née Bagguley. The pair had travelled down to Wembley together for the 50th anniversary celebrations, and she was particularly thrilled that her father – aged 93 – was able to be there with them. Finally he saw his daughter recognised for all the work she had put in and what she had achieved half a century previously.

'He was a footballer himself, bless him, and I've got three brothers, so obviously as a kid if I played out, it was with the lads, so it was football [I played],' Bagguley recalled. 'My mum, she was thrilled to bits in the end when I got in the England squad, but when I was very young she used to go mad, because I'd go out, play football, come back after, and I'd send my brother in first and say, "Get Mum talking so I can get past her!" One particular Sunday I remember she caught me and she went mad – "Just look at the state of you! You're supposed to be a young lady! You get in that bath and get changed!"

'I got in the bath, and when I came out there was a kilt skirt and a little jumper laying on the bed.

'"What are they?"

'She said, "Put them on."

'"I'm not putting that on!"

'She said, "You are, or you won't play out."

'I said, "I won't play out then. I'm not going out in that!"'

Bagguley's football career very nearly foundered before it even started. The women's team that she and some other young women started in their home town of Buxton did not enjoy a successful inaugural season; in fact, their first was also their last. She had done enough against Macclesfield in a resounding thrashing – one she recalls as resulting in a 36-0 scoreline – to impress them, though, and their club founder Veronica Bailey asked her to join them for the next campaign in 1970. At the age of 15, though, Bagguley was not able to drive herself the 24-mile round trip; instead, the Macclesfield players arranged to pick her up and drop her off. By the age of 17, she was invited to Loughborough for the first ever England trials, under the watchful gaze of manager Eric Worthington.

'He was a real nice bloke, he really was, full of encouragement,' recalled Bagguley. 'At that point, sometimes in the papers they were ... not slagging us off, but taking the mickey a little bit. He always backed us.'

On 18 November 1972, at Ravenscraig Stadium in Greenock, Worthington selected Bagguley as one of the 11 England players who started their first official international against Scotland. It was a far cry from the lush, smooth grass adorning Wembley, graced by the modern-day Lionesses.

'The pitch was horrendous – most men would refuse to play on it without a doubt,' said Bagguley, 'and it was so cold. It was bitterly cold.'

Nevertheless, she still treasures the special memories of that day; as with most other international footballers, she vividly remembers lining up to hear the national anthem being played.

'I used to be so nervous before the match,' she admitted. 'Football boots then had proper studs in them. I remember going to the toilet and I could hear my feet clattering on the floor, shaking. But the minute you got on the pitch, that all went.'

Bagguley's England career lasted around six years; using up her entire holiday allocation from work for football became less and less appealing as she got older.

'All my mates were going off to Spain for a holiday that year, and I was that little bit older and I really wanted to go on holiday, so I didn't go that year for the England trials,' she said with a smile. 'I'd had fabulous times with them, been abroad, in France, in Holland, in Switzerland.'

She carried on playing for Macclesfield until she and her husband decided to start a family in 1984, and the arrival of daughter Zoe. She did not regret her relatively early retirement, and remained involved with local football teams, and although her daughter had never wanted to play the game, Bagguley also had a hope for the future when it came to the next generation.

'I've got two granddaughters: one is very much into netball, and the younger one, she's only three, she's got one hell of a kick on her! I'm hoping she might come through at some point.'

Bagguley's daughter, Zoe Taylor, was well aware of her mother's intention to introduce what she called 'Nanna's training' for little Olive at some point.

'My mum is determined for one of us to be a footballer!' she laughed. 'Olive loves playing, and Mum's like, "She's a proper leftie, she's got a right boot on her when she goes for it!"'

Older daughter Ella had loved watching the Lionesses' success in 2022, and been amazed and thrilled to see her grandmother hailed as a sporting pioneer – particularly enjoying the television coverage.

'When they played the USA and the day where they've gone down there to get her cap and they were there on the pitch, the guard of honour, I found that really special for Ella,' said Taylor, 'because it was like, "Oh my God, there's Nanna!"

'There was this shot where my mum was holding her shirt up and it said "Bagguley" on the back and she was like, "Pause the telly, Mum!" It was a really big thing for her to see it as well. My youngest daughter, she's too young. She doesn't really understand but obviously we've recorded it so we'll be able to show her. If that hadn't been celebrated now, then we wouldn't have been able to be a part of that.

'It was nice for my mum's dad because he's still around, and he was the one who was driving to training and driving them to games – they were the ones who put the effort into it for her to get where she was. For him to be able to go down with her and see that, that was really special. Mum's got both sides: we're seeing it, and supporting her, and then there's my dad and my grandad.'

Taylor had also taken great pleasure in seeing her mother reunited with team-mates, many of whom she had lost touch with since hanging up her boots. Meeting up with them again had jogged plenty of memories, and Bagguley had enjoyed regaling her daughter with tales of matches, away trips and training camps.

'I think they were rum 'uns!' she laughed. 'A lot of them she'd not spoken to for a long time. It's just been really nice for her to meet up with them again and rekindle those friendships because nowadays with social media you can keep on top of that with people who don't necessarily live so local. It's been a really special time for her and we've loved it, loved watching it.'

Taylor had always been aware that her mum had been a footballer, but as a child she did not realise quite what a big deal it should or could be.

'She'd talked about it and kept this scrapbook with newspaper cuttings. I suppose it was always kind of a thing, but it never was really a big thing. I'd say to friends, "Oh yeah, my mum used to play football. She was in the England women's team." And they'd be like, "Oh, that's amazing."

'But I think because of this year with how the team did in the Euros, she's now getting a bit more recognition, and actually, it's a really big thing. It's something to be really proud of. I think society didn't really appreciate that before. Back then when she played, it wasn't a big thing. It wasn't televised like it is now, they didn't have the crowds like they have now. It's nice for her to feel that they were part of the journey.'

* * *

Kerry Davis, the first woman of black heritage to play for the official England team, was inducted into the National Football Museum Hall of Fame the week before the celebrations at Wembley. The panel had voted unanimously to add her to the roll of honour, in recognition of her long and illustrious career – 16 years as an international, with 82 caps and 44 goals, including appearing in the inaugural 1984 UEFA Championships Final, and later at the Women's World Cup in 1995.

Now 60 years old, she told reporters on the evening that watching England win the Euros made her instantly wonder what the impact would be for the next generations of female footballers.

'"Finally, women's football is going to be respected." Those were my first thoughts,' she said to the press.

'When I played I paid to play football. Everybody volunteered, whether it be the coaches, the manager, now it's just like a world away to what I was used to. The TV channels were not interested. The newspapers were not interested. If local players were playing for England, you'd get the local papers that would show a little bit and put the score in but it was a battle. There was nothing, no real sponsorship – nothing. It was hard work all the way through, that's the only way you could describe it. We loved to play football and that was the enjoyable thing. We could just put that stuff to the side and go [and] play football and enjoy it.

'It's taken longer than I thought it would to get to here but I'm very, very happy that it's got here. My generation and the generation before me have been waiting a long time for this to explode and to be on the back pages.'

The generations afterwards felt the same. Karen Farley, a forward eight years Davis's junior, had played alongside her for England for a few years, and had a similar perspective to the players who had gone before her.

'We've never had anything, we never had any attention, especially from the media or any sort of attention apart from within our own group,' she said. 'I'm just so honoured that they finally actually recognised that there was life before the [2022] Euros, and the Euros didn't just happen, that it's decades and decades of hard work and sacrifice from everyone that was involved, not only the players but parents. My parents used to run me around all of the south-east of England. All the years of that input is what has made women's football actually carry on and has created that platform for the Euros to happen.

'There was no expectation [of recognition]. I know of players that are very bitter and were like, "Well, I'm not going, because it's too little too late," and it's like, "OK, that's your prerogative." I think they could have easily ignored it. They could easily have just gone, "This is what's happening now. Don't worry about what happened before." They had a choice to make, and thankfully they made that choice that included all of us and gave us all that acknowledgement.'

Farley had gone years without even thinking about her football career, despite having played at a World Cup. She had even uprooted her life and headed to Sweden to join a club there, which shaped the rest of her life off the pitch too as she learnt the language and stepped into a new career in the British embassy there. It was not until some years later, back in the UK and starting a family, that she even mentioned it, when she began to meet new people.

'They asked for my story: "Where do you come from? What do you do?" And that comes into the conversation and people were like, "Are you serious? You played for England? And you don't talk about it?"

'For us to have to have that opportunity, I think it was fantastic. It was those few weeks when it was all the hype leading up to the USA game. It was so exciting – it certainly made me feel very special.'

Farley was coached in Sweden by the legendary Pia Sundhage, who had been part of the national team who won the first-ever official UEFA European tournament for women back in 1984, beating England in the final. Much of what Farley saw from Sarina Wiegman reminded her of Sundhage's style and manner.

'It's that real driving force,' she said. 'They have something inside them that is just football pumping through their veins.

'Sarina came in and basically gave the girls the confidence to be who they really are, and to concentrate, and to forget all of the stereotypes, to forget all of the restrictions that we've lived under for so many years. Just forget about that. This is your opportunity. Be yourselves.

'And there was almost like a little switch clicked in them, which made them just leave everything at the front door, and just go out on that pitch.'

Farley had watched plenty of the documentaries and news items that had started to proliferate after the tournament, and had been impressed by the team spirit that she could see emanating from each member of the squad.

'I think she's driven that into them,' she said. 'I think it was always there – but we're English, aren't we? We're very demure, and we don't want to take space, and we don't want to be too cocky, and we don't want to be too flashy. She has instilled in them that attitude, that killer winning attitude: "Listen, you're here. You are here with this opportunity to change women's football forever." And that is what they did.

'It still makes me tear up when I think about what they've done. Without her, we would have got maybe to the semis, we would have maybe got to the final but we would have lost again, because we never go that whole way. Her way of leadership has just changed our game forever.'

Farley had taken her wife and children to the USA friendly with her, and had noticed her young daughter becoming more and more interested in her football career – even regularly searching the internet for her mother's name to see if she could find out any new information about her. Even her son's new friends at secondary school had seen Farley and her family on the local news ahead of the USA friendly, and had been suitably impressed. She felt like winning the Euros and the subsequent recognition of the previous generations was like a fairy tale, and she was glad not just for the acknowledgement of people's hard work, but also because she got to thank some individuals who had had a huge impact on her life, sometimes without even knowing.

'When we went down to Wembley for the USA game, we were all there, but the 1972 team, those women are just stood there and when they all came out because they got their caps, it was just beautiful. It was so beautiful, because they had it even worse than we had it. I started playing in the 1980s, so they were ten years before me, and I know how hard it was in the 1980s to play football. I know the crap that we had to take. How we stuck it out I really don't know.

'But to see them get that acknowledgement, I hope that the people who arranged it understand how important that was for every one of those players that were there, every one of those players that turned up that night. It was beautiful walking around that bar – all you could hear was squeals of excitement. I met Jane Stanley when I was 16 and I got taken to my very first senior training camp at Loughborough. We were all on camp beds in a sports hall: Gill Coultard, Hope Powell, Brenda Sempare, Marieanne Spacey, Debbie Bampton, all of these players that were the best. They were our icons, they were superhuman. I was quite a confident young girl, but I was still shitting myself! And I remember Jane Stanley took me under her wing – "Come on, come and have the camp bed next to me." She looked after me, and she'd obviously forgotten about that.

'I went up to her [at Wembley] and I was like, "I will never forget how you looked after me in our training session that weekend because I was completely out of my depth and didn't know anyone." It was such a long time ago, but that memory still sticks in my head.'

She also had the fondest of memories of the summer, when so many former players had been welcomed to the England training camp. Having had no female footballing role models of her own as a child – instead donning a replica Liverpool kit in honour of their Scottish superstar Kenny Dalglish – she was still slightly incredulous to see the number of little girls with their own England shirts emblazoned with the names of Alessia Russo or Beth Mead.

'When we went down to that training session, there's always that element of, "You're in the presence of someone that's done something amazing,"' said Farley with a grin. 'But at the end of the day, they are just another human being just like all of us. I remember I was really nervous! I was thinking that they probably think, "We've got to do this, we've got to meet the old ones." But it really wasn't like that.'

She enjoyed a chat with centre-half and vice-captain Millie Bright, which stood out in her mind.

'I said, "Thank you so much for doing this today."

'She replied, "What are you talking about? If it wasn't for you lot, we wouldn't be here." And it actually felt genuine. It didn't just feel like that's one of the things that they've been media-trained to say! It felt like she meant it. And it was really lovely.'

Of course, the Lionesses were continuing to live their ideals publicly, not simply murmuring platitudes off-camera. With new prime minister Liz Truss in place, they continued to press her to commit to investment in girls' grassroots and schools football. They used their match against the Czech Republic in Brighton to promote their 'Let Girls Play' campaign, pushing for every girl to have equal access to football in their school and community. The squad warmed up wearing special logoed t-shirts with the campaign name, with coach Sarina Wiegman donning a pin badge throughout the match.

At the training camp beforehand, at the Lensbury resort in south-west London, the newly installed premier had met with the squad and posed for photos, although she did not take any questions from the attending members of the media. She also had a private meeting with captain Leah Williamson and defender Lotte Wubben-Moy, who was the driving force behind the Lionesses' initial letter and the trigger to the 'Let Girls Play' initiative.

'You don't get these moments very often,' said Baroness Sue Campbell, the FA's director of women's football, speaking to the press afterwards. 'These are iconic moments and I think this is a group of players who are really very committed to this legacy. This is not something they're doing as a nice thing, this is something they care passionately about and they have every intention of following this through. So just like on the pitch they're not going to take no for an answer.'

Campbell did, however, agree that little change had been evident thus far since the summer despite the huge numbers of girls and women wanting to play football.

'We at the Football Association have put quite a big investment into school sport and club sport for youngsters and what we are seeing is massive demand coming through the door. So we're seeing lots of people wanting to play the game; we just want to make sure the opportunity is equal to the demand.'

4

Sustainable

SHELLY PROVAN had played all around England, gracing teams at the highest level, gaining international recognition. If one were to ask the full-back herself how she had achieved such success, she would demur, brushing off the suggestion that she was one of the most talented footballers of her generation, and instead pointing to her undeniable work ethic. Through almost the entirety of her playing career, Provan balanced football with her job as a PE teacher, and latterly added the responsibilities of a mother of two to the mix. Although it would be impossible to doubt the commitment of a woman who would finish her day's work and drive from Southampton to train with Doncaster Rovers Belles multiple times a week, her ability could not be refuted.

She started her career with Southampton, and when she returned to her home-town club in 2018, she must have thought that this would be the place she would end her career, bringing everything full circle. This version of Southampton was a little different to the one she had known as a younger player; this was a club ready to put significant backing and infrastructure in place to support its women's team, one that was considering the possibility of stepping up into the elite tiers and moving towards professionalism for its players.

Provan had never really been able to consider playing as a full-time professional before; with a small family to look after, plus the understandable safety net of a reliable teacher's salary, the demands of a footballer's life simply could not be entertained. But by 2022, with Provan having enjoyed her spell as Southampton's club captain and with the club set to step up into the Women's Championship, the situation had changed. She and her husband discussed whether it might be feasible for her to stay with the club in the second tier and become a full-time professional with the rest of the squad, and agreed it was a possibility.

Provan's dreams were smashed, though. She was informed towards the end of the season that she was not going to be retained for the coming campaign. It was tough news to take, and after leaving the club, the 38-year-old was wondering what she would do next. Perhaps, she thought, it was time to finally hang up her boots.

'I didn't want to speak to anybody,' she admitted. 'I was contemplating retiring. My husband almost wanted me to retire, because the commitment for him is quite a lot, but he knew that there was always going to be something – even if it wasn't football, I'd be doing something else. I can't not exercise. I joined a running club, and I was talking about doing CrossFit, and he said, "If you're going to be out two or three nights a week doing things like that anyway, you might as well be playing football, because that's where you're happiest.'" Provan heard that Oxford United might be interested in signing her. She knew their manager Liam Gilbert, having grown up in the same part of the world, and despite feeling somewhat bruised by the way she had left Southampton, she took his call and agreed to go along to one of his training sessions.

'The rest is history, really,' she said. She agreed to join them for 2022/23, announcing the move in July, and attributed much of the decision to the support that Gilbert had offered her. 'He's been incredible. I think we're lucky to have him in the women's game, to be honest.'

With the benefit of some months' distance, Provan realised she wanted to end her footballing career on her own terms, not someone else's; she felt almost as if she had been nudged towards deciding to retire, and she refused to let that happen.

'I'd dipped into those thoughts [about retirement], and almost being at that point was, yeah, a little bit scary!' she admitted. 'When you think about it, it's all I've ever done, really, since I was young. The only seasons I've had out were from my knee [ligament injury] and having the kids, and even then it was just focused on getting back on the pitch again, so [retirement] was a strange thought.

'When I get there, I'll know. Speaking to others who have got to that point, I think you yourself know that it's time. Hopefully that's how I'll feel.'

She might also have considered playing football at a lower, local league level, but she felt she had more to give.

'I could have just played when I wanted, trained when I wanted, but I still had that hunger to play at a higher level while my body could still cope,' she said. 'I'll keep going. We'll see what happens this season, we'll see what happens in Oxford and what happens with the league and take it from there ... again.'

Oxford had recently increased their training requirements to three nights a week; Provan agreed to commit to two. The travel was not quite as demanding as her younger years driving from Hampshire to Yorkshire, and her children were now old enough to appreciate a football match as well as their mother's career.

'They were quite upset when I left Saints – my son cried, bless him,' she recalled. 'It was getting to that point where it was cool with his friends that I played for Saints. When I first started playing for them, he didn't really care, he couldn't give two hoots!

'The children are very keen on coming to watch [Oxford] – they are already on board! We're trying to get them Oxford kits. It's a bit harder to get them to the game, they've got their own sports commitments over the weekend, but I think they'll come to the odd few. It's nice to have them when they're there.'

Provan laughed self-deprecatingly when considering the question of whether she might end up becoming a 'sports mum', content to cheer on her children from the sidelines and living a little vicariously.

'I should say yes! I love watching them play and they both play football and rugby and tennis at the moment. My husband helps run my son's football team, and I did a little bit of coaching with that team – I might end up going into more of the coaching side of things.' She paused briefly, her train of thought once again turning to her life after football. 'While I'm playing, I find it hard to get my head around using that time to coach. I'd rather be out there doing at the moment. Perhaps that mentality will change.'

* * *

'She's such a great role model,' said Oxford United manager Liam Gilbert of his new signing. 'She takes her time in between drills or at the end of practice to talk to the younger ones. We've got a 16-year-old full-back, and Shelly has just taken her under her wing. She offers advice and is there as a bit of a sounding board for someone who we think has got a really high ceiling. To have someone like that, it makes my life a lot easier – let's be honest, she's going to listen to Shelly a lot more than she's going to listen to me, isn't she? As much as I'd like to think differently, we all know that's the case – because I'd probably be doing the same!'

At the start of the 2022/23 season, Gilbert had been at Oxford United for seven years. The first two years of his tenure were as the development team manager, and he stepped up to manage the first team after their demotion out of what was then Women's Super League 2 at the end of 2017/18. They had finished eighth in a ten-team division, but were relegated due to the league's restructure, as they had not obtained a licence to enable them to compete in the newly rebranded Women's Championship. Nor had Watford, who finished bottom – or the league champions, Doncaster Rovers Belles. (Fifth-placed Sheffield did achieve a licence before deciding not to compete in the second tier.)

Oxford had been rather reticent about applying for the licence in the first place. The club did not submit an application for the first round of the process, in November 2017, saying in a statement then: 'We are committed to investing in and developing Oxford United WFC but we are awaiting further information on the composition and structure of the competition.' By March 2018, the second opportunity to put in a bid, the club had received the assurances they wanted, reviewing their financial situation and pulling together a plan with the proposed intent of becoming a full-time club in the top division within the next five years. That would have, obviously, required additional financial support, with the men's club chairman Darryl Eales agreeing to continue his backing.

On receiving the news of the demotion in May 2018, United's managing director Niall McWilliams said in a statement that it was a 'great opportunity to take stock'.

'The model we believe works best is a team that allows the best women players in the county to play at the highest level and work with the best coaches to develop their game,' he added. 'That then helps to continue the development of the women's game all across Oxfordshire.'

He may well have been right, with a sensible Plan B following such a disappointment. However, the WSL2 was a semi-professional league, with players and staff committed to the club as part of their career trajectory. Removing that element to compete in the third tier – even though it could be the best move long-term for the infrastructure of women's football across the county – meant that a lot of people had no choice but to leave. Gilbert, however, was one of the few who did not.

'When we got demoted, everyone left apart from me,' explained Gilbert wryly, 'so I was left to pick up the pieces and rebuild us as a club in tier three.'

That was not an exaggeration.

'There were a lot of people that lost their careers, if you like: we had a general manager, two full-time coaches, a full-time head of marketing who was one of our players, so it's quite hard to see those bits fall around you. It makes you realise how fickle and how tough an industry we work in, because it's just like that: you can lose your job without necessarily doing anything wrong.'

Gilbert was a part-time member of staff, balancing it with his full-time job as a teacher, which gave him some degree of practice at the kind of pastoral care needed to approach the players coming to terms with the loss of their immediate semi-professional prospects with Oxford.

'I reached out to players to see if they were OK, to tell them we still support them: I had two respond,' he recalled. 'That was how it started. We managed to keep six or seven in the end, but a lot of them were the fringe players, in the development team. Then we had a few very good youngsters who had the opportunity to come through [into the first team].'

That kind of optimism was characteristic of the way Gilbert described that time in the life of the club.

'It was quite interesting,' he said. 'I was in a fortunate position. I got the opportunity to pick the pieces up, which I know is a positive picture from a massive negative, but from a very selfish point of view I've been allowed to build a football club how I see one should run, could run.'

That included pastoral care, for which Gilbert had a very clear philosophy, and from which Provan said she benefited hugely.

'I reach out to every player separately once every two or three weeks just to see how they are,' he said. 'I don't know that we would be where we are if I didn't try and do stuff like that, I don't think the players would buy in to myself or to the club to start with or commit the way they do, necessarily. I could be completely wrong, but I notice the difference with players the more you get to know them, how they act with you.

'That's our job as managers. To get the best out of the person as a footballer, you have to know the person to know the best way to motivate them and push them. It's really important we know what's going on with her, take all of it in to make sure that we can support people in the best way. I know from my work in school, mental health is such an important thing, and because of how Covid had an effect on people's lives, I still think we're seeing people suffer with certain issues, especially in social situations. We've got 17- and 18-year-olds coming through that spent that period of their life just glued to a computer screen, not really interacting with people, so they can come across a bit abrupt because for two years of their lives, that's all they knew.'

Oxford United adjusted well, despite the turnover in playing staff, finishing fourth then third in their next two league seasons. In 2019/20 and 2020/21, the FA Women's National League suffered from two consecutive curtailments because of Covid-induced season suspensions. By the 2021/22 season, Gilbert had steered Oxford United straight again. They finished second in the FA Women's National League Southern Division, nine points behind runaway leaders Southampton, who ultimately won the national play-off to step up into the Women's Championship.

Gilbert was ready for his team to finally go one better and win the league, and had been pleased with what he had seen early in the 2022/23 season.

'We didn't know what we were going to get after last year, after taking Southampton so close,' he said. 'We actually lost quite a few players: we lost nine players with retirements and relocations, so to bring in nine new players and have them gel so quickly … we looked at people as opposed to players first this year, and it's had a massive difference.

'Shelly – she's an unbelievable person. It's made such a difference off the pitch which has translated on it, and everyone else we've brought in is the same. They're good people.'

Gilbert had known Provan for a very long time. Her father had been his coach when he first started playing senior football as a teenager, and she had occasionally joined the squad for pre-season training.

'She was unbelievable – she was the best player by an absolute mile,' he grinned. He later played Sunday league football with her brother, and stayed in touch with the whole family. 'They're really nice people.'

Of course, Gilbert saw in the summer of 2022 that Provan had been released by Southampton. He had been surprised by the timing, so early in the close season, and had heard on the football grapevine she intended to retire; it would explain why she had left a club she had been with for such a long time and with whom she had bought into the long-term vision so entirely. It was a colleague at another club who told him that was not the case at all. He wanted to see whether she was interested in signing for his team, although he knew that after such a disappointment she was still likely to feel very down.

'When I had a chat with her, I said, "Listen, I know things haven't been the way they had been for you, or ended how you wanted them to – come into a training session to see how you find it, see how you find the girls and we can have a chat, see if you want to carry on playing,"' he said. 'I left it with the ball in her court, and she came in [to training]. After one session, she was like, "I love this, it's great, this is what I need."

'We got a bit lucky with timing, to get someone like her on board. Because of knowing her and knowing what happened, we were able to handle the situation well and to support her in the best way possible.'

Having a player like Provan alongside his promising youngsters plus those with less first-team experience was crucial, not just for the short term but as Gilbert and the club began to plan for the future. In contrast to their situation when they were mulling over whether a life in the Women's Super League set-up was the right move for them, Oxford United were prepared to step up to the challenge in years to come.

'We've had full backing by the [main men's] club and the board for the last two years; the club's new ownership that came in about 18 months ago have really supported everything we've done and have allowed us to grow,' explained Gilbert. 'My big thing is to make sure we can grow and be sustainable. I know a lot of teams have just chucked money at certain areas, but I don't see the point in that, because we worked so hard to rebuild the football club. If we were to throw wages and everything at the club, [then] our players this year didn't get promoted and then the money is taken away, we're probably fighting relegation [the season afterwards], whereas we've just had a general manager appointed, which has been massive. It's a part-time role, but it's a massive step, and we just want to make sure that we're building. I want to bring the youth players through. Our talent centre is very successful – I'm going to watch one of our girls play for England [junior team] today – and we've got a load of talented players like that coming through.

'I think they will be the future, because in five years' time, when there is big money in the women's game' – Gilbert paused here and corrected himself with a grin, reflecting on the summer's development – 'or bigger money in the women's game, that's how we're going to have to compete – by trusting our own processes.'

In the meantime, his task was to continue the challenging job of tier three management, weaving together a squad ranging from schoolgirls hoping for a professional career in football to the international experience of Provan, via those happy to play at a semi-professional level but prioritising their day job off the pitch. It took all Gilbert's skills as a coach, plus his teaching experience, plus some diplomacy on the side.

'There's a lot to think about,' he said. 'It does take a lot to get used to, if I'm honest. If they've had a bad day at work and they're not training very well and you want to lose your head [with them], it might be outside factors that are controlling it.

'I'd probably compare it to what the men's Conference [league] was like, where you had 24 teams all fighting for one position or two positions now. It's exactly the same here. You've got a lot of younger kids that want to play professionally now, because they see it as a career and there's the ability to earn a good wage. You've got the senior players that have got careers and they don't want to go into football full-time. That's quite an interesting balance, trying to keep those players on the same sort of page and committed in the same ways. We have an optional session with the men's first-team manager, and all the younger players are there every single week. And they can't understand why the older players don't go.'

Although the club was stable, Gilbert still was not in a position to offer long-term contracts to players, so in lieu of giving them that kind of financial carrot, he worked on making the sessions as enjoyable as possible for them.

'You are just relying on building a relationship with players and then trusting in your ability and enjoying the environment,' he said. 'We're spending six to ten hours a week together and if they don't enjoy what they're doing, they're not going to come back anyway, so that's been quite an important thing – and one we've learnt about over time. The last thing I want is a player coming to training and thinking, "Oh, I've got to come here again."'

* * *

Tom Peevor had similar considerations at Shrewsbury Town, promoted to the West Midlands Regional Women's Football League Premier Division from the Division One North at the end of the 2021/22 season. His side, now in the fifth tier of the pyramid, fell under the auspices of the men's club's community foundation, and he had been there for just over four years – two of which he had spent as manager. When he had first taken the post of assistant manager, the team's mindset was a very amateur one, and working with foundation chief executive Jamie Edwards, a new path for women's football began to be forged.

'When the women's team came under our banner, we wanted it to be done properly,' explained Edwards. 'We've done that. We use some of our full-time staff to deliver on it, have a pathway of the emerging talent centre, and [we are] wholeheartedly trying to make it sustainable.'

For Shrewsbury, sustainability was not just about relying on subsidies from the men's club. Edwards and the rest of the staff were keen to build attendances and look at commercial opportunities such as merchandising, just as a men's team would. It was also about ensuring the team itself was sustainable, with a talent pathway from junior age groups to the senior squad, plus coaches and backroom staff developing there as well.

'When we first started, there was no kind of joined-up thinking,' Peevor said. 'Over the years – and it's made my job a lot easier – the support from the foundation has been amazing in terms of giving us a clear direction, the structure around the team, to enable me to help the players ultimately.'

Peevor's players had also benefited from being linked to the club's community foundation. They made personal appearances at schools and grassroots clubs, giving girls local role models.

'We're far more accessible than the men's team, for example,' he said, 'so we're really trying to use that as a platform to help inspire more girls to get involved in the game and we think it's possible to do that.'

That visibility in the local area was not something the club had forced on the players; it was something they had lobbied for themselves.

'A lot of teams will sit at the start of the season and go, "Right, we're going to go for promotion," or "We're going to go for this kind of position,"' said Peevor, 'but a lot of what we talk about is there's a bigger meaning to our team, really. Yes, we want to get promoted and do well, but they want to be role models within the local community, in every aspect.

'We talked about what our habits are, in training, on matchdays, but also outside of that and what we do. If you see our social media, you'll see that everything aligns with being a role model. We've done stuff where we've highlighted what our players actually do as a day job, because sometimes I do think people forget that these women have jobs!'

Essentially, Shrewsbury Town were working to build as professional a structure as possible for their women's team, while acknowledging that the chances of them turning professional as a club were limited – certainly for the time being.

'If we get promoted a league, we are in the fourth tier of English women's football,' said Edwards. 'The fourth tier of

English football for the men is professional and there'd be hefty fines if you're pulling out of games at the last minute or going to play in the FA Cup on pretty much a park pitch – it just wouldn't happen. The clubs that are trying to do it properly should be recognised.'

Shrewsbury had applied for promotion a few years previously, when the league had restructured, but they had been turned down. Some of the clubs whose applications had been accepted were now either no longer playing at that level, or no longer in existence. It made Edwards and Peevor even more committed to ensure their own infrastructure was sound; Edwards was concerned that clubs that were taking steps to prepare for promotion were not being adequately supported in the amateur set-up, and that this would result in clubs ultimately becoming frustrated with their failure to see any progress.

On a more immediate level, Peevor was encountering challenges presented by the differing levels of semi-professionalism within the new league, and wondered whether some of his team's results that season might have been partly attributable to late-notice postponements and a subsequent loss of momentum.

'It can be really tough,' he admitted. He now had a plan in place if a match was called off at the last minute, whether that was calling the squad in for an extra training session or arranging a friendly match, but also acknowledged that he had to use all his interpersonal skills to ensure players felt supported and connected to the club, particularly in periods where they did not have matches every week. 'It's important that the players know I'm there to listen if they've got any concerns. They do get opportunities, whether it's as a group or individually to say how they're feeling and then I can talk to them.'

Peevor was helped by having two other coaches working alongside him, including a new female first-team coach. 'Female coaches have been really hard to find!' he said. 'I've not seen any other club in this situation around us really, being so lucky to have that kind of staffing. It's meant that I can have those one-to-one chats which can be really hard because these players are coming straight from work, straight from college, uni, straight to a training session, but having that staffing structure has helped me to check in with players, and it's definitely needed when things are chopping around during the season.'

Despite the postponements, Shrewsbury had made it into the first round proper of the Women's FA Cup, and had been rewarded with possibly the toughest draw they could have had – a home tie against third-tier Wolverhampton Wanderers, top of the FA Women's National League Northern Premier Division.

'I'm personally in it for these games,' smiled Peevor. 'This excites me much more than going to a team that's a league below us, so we're really looking forward to playing it and just seeing where we're at against them. We've got a plan and we're going to work on it and embrace the challenge.'

WINTER

5

Voice

WITH THE top leagues of the men's game on a break to enable players to take part in the World Cup in Qatar – scheduled in December rather than the usual summer slot, which in that part of the world would prove prohibitively hot – leading female players were outspoken about the optics of hosting a World Cup in that particular place, a country that had attracted criticism for its treatment of migrant workers as well as women and LGBTQ+ people.

'It's a tragedy. We've lost so many workers' lives,' Lionesses captain Leah Williamson told the *Evening Standard* newspaper. 'There are issues surrounding a community that I am part of, I live it every day with my team-mates. I have a team with a same-sex couple in it. How can I be in support of something that wishes for them to stay away or not be who they are?'

Her Arsenal and England team-mate Lotte Wubben-Moy agreed, telling reporters: 'As an England team we all have strong values and a lot of those values aren't reflected, in the way that we see it, in Qatar.'

FIFA president Gianni Infantino and secretary general Fatma Samoura wrote to all the competing teams ahead of the tournament, apparently asking them to avoid commenting on such issues, which they described as 'ideological or political', and instead concentrate solely on football.

'We know football does not live in a vacuum and we are equally aware that there are many challenges and difficulties of a political nature all around the world,' they wrote. 'But please do not allow football to be dragged into every ideological or political battle that exists.'

Some teams had planned a protest of sorts at the tournament, with the captains of England, Wales, Belgium, Denmark, Germany, the Netherlands and Switzerland all intending to wear a rainbow-coloured armband with the slogan 'One Love', highlighting a message of LGBTQ+ equality. However, they were warned that they could face bookings or being asked to leave the pitch, and opted not to take a stand in that particular way. However, former Lioness Alex Scott, working for the BBC during the tournament, wore the armband during broadcasts. Her book, *How (Not) To Be Strong*, had recently been released, in which she discussed her personal life, including a relationship with then-team-mate Kelly Smith.

Seeing the World Cup unfolding in Qatar gave Lewes CEO Maggie Murphy plenty to think about. She attributed her job and the way her life had progressed almost entirely to FIFA's decision to award the tournament to that country. With a background in anti-corruption, she had watched FIFA executives become embroiled in various legal cases, and she followed it carefully, with her anger growing at every step.

The money swilling around in elite men's football could, and should, have been used so much more wisely in women's football, she thought. She decided to channel that anger for change. She was part of the creation of Equal Playing Field, a grassroots initiative to challenge sex inequality in sport, which raised the profile of the campaign with impressive, record-breaking challenges around the world: in 2017, the football match played at the highest altitude, at Mount Kilimanjaro in Tanzania, followed by the lowest altitude match ever the year after, at the Dead Sea in Jordan.

'I've tried to be part of the solution rather than part of the problem,' she said. That did not mean she ever thought that she would go into football administration. 'If I'd just been allowed to play football and had been given decent opportunities, I would never be the CEO of a football club. All I wanted to do was play. I really wanted it to be just something I did at the weekend.

'I do have this justness and this fairness that runs through me, and my world was in anti-corruption, human rights, working with governments around the world, businesses around the world, living overseas, so I was never meaning to be in football.'

It was by chance that Murphy noticed Lewes and their work for equality. A couple of months after the record-breaking match at the top of Kilimanjaro, she saw this independent football club in Sussex posting on social media about its decision to pay its male and female players equally, and asking for people to buy into the club and become an 'owner'. Murphy clicked and paid.

'At the time, I thought that was my act of support, like an act of resistance,' she said. 'I remember saying to myself, "I'll probably never go there."'

'I probably pronounced it "Lose FC",' she added with a smile.

But as part of Equal Playing Field, promoting equality in football, her path kept on crossing with Lewes, a club that was doing the same. She got to know some of the board of directors, and was then approached in early 2019 to invite her to join the club as the women's team's general manager.

'My reaction at the time was, "No, I don't think you understand – I'm on the outside! This is my angry space, this is my campaigning space, but I have a career over here!"

'And then the more that I thought about it, the more I realised that I was being asked to put my money where my mouth was, and in the way that I was asking others to put their money where their mouth was, I had to do the same myself. So I took the leap to become [women's] general manager, did that for two years, and then the club asked me to take over the men's side as well as the women's side.'

Sitting in her office – a portable cabin – she admitted that she sometimes wondered what she would be doing if she had turned that offer down.

'I know that at the time I was getting a little bit antsy in my previous role,' she reflected, 'like I needed to be fired up again. I felt that I'd done my time in the stuff that I had been doing. Lots of different things all crashed at the same time, and that threw up this opportunity which in many ways I was nuts to take. Financially it was a very difficult, very bad decision. But the way that I want to pour myself into stuff in my life, then I think it was the right thing to do.'

When Lewes had initially announced their policy of pay equality, they expected other clubs to follow suit. Murphy acknowledged that such a bold decision did require bravery, and it did require thinking about football and its structures in entirely new ways; challenging the system in a tangible fashion is not always an easy thing to do.

'We really don't want to be holier than thou, which I think is something I'm very conscious of,' she said. 'What we don't want to be is like a goody-two-shoes, always banging on about equality.

'But yeah, [committing to equality] genuinely is really hard to do. Sometimes I get bored of some of the questions people say – when they're asking the wrong questions. They're like, "What are you doing?" [and should be asking] not just the "how" and the challenges, but, "What are the threats to it?" because there's loads and loads of threats around it as well.'

Murphy was honest; trailblazing is tough, especially when it feels like you are out on a limb, running a football club for men and women with both given equal weighting. Many potential investors were only interested in the huge untapped resources of women's sport, wondering if it might be possible to start a new, exciting, glamorous women's football franchise like Angel City in the USA, the club with a majority female ownership group including actress Natalie Portman and tennis legend Serena Williams. Murphy half-laughed as she said that sometimes she wished she was running a club that only catered for half of the population.

'The reason that we're special is because of that equality,' she said, 'because it is bloody hard, and it is difficult to pull some elements of the men's side forward. When we do bring on partners or sponsors, a lot of the time we might say, "Oh, it's because of the women's side." But actually I think a lot of the time it's because of our equality side. It's not because we're a great women's team. It's because we're doing something with equality, and equality doesn't mean women, equality means men and women. So sometimes I have to correct myself, or I have to correct other people around me that talk about "we're making more money because of the women's side" – it's actually because of equality, and equality is both.'

Of course, Murphy laced her hypothetical quote from her hypothetical interlocuter with a great deal of irony. Such arguments have been used for many decades by football clubs looking for a way to save expense – and who thus decide to close down their provision for women, because the men are more profitable, attracting more television broadcasting money and more sponsorship, and because the men are higher up in the pyramid, training more often. Lewes's situation reversed the position, but Murphy thought it was no less dangerous and no more logical.

'We cannot use the same language to justify promoting the women because that's exactly the same language that's been used to hold them back as well,' she argued. 'Just because we're in a unique space doesn't mean that we should fall into that trap, I think.'

With women's football in England still governed by a licensing system, Lewes were considering applying for a licence to compete in the top tier – not necessarily because they expected to be promoted in the very near future, but as a benchmarking process, to see how they were progressing compared to other clubs, and how much further they would need to go. Murphy wondered whether this might actually highlight some future challenges for the club.

'Money solves everything,' she said. 'The things that we would find the hardest to realise are things like full-time salaries for the players, but that's just money. It's not our ground. It's not our people. It's not a structural thing. It's just money. And I think money is the hardest thing, but it's also the easiest thing. We're currently looking at potential ways to raise money, differently and uniquely. We can't generate enough money at the moment from the classic places, sponsorship and matchday revenue. We have to think differently.

'We're constantly trying to be innovative: how the hell do we make enough money to stop ourselves from being swallowed up by clubs that have not done the hard work, but who are now receiving just a greater slide of money across the table from the men's side of the club? My biggest fear, or my biggest wish, I don't know, is that we're very careful in the governance in the licence criteria that we apply, that doesn't from the top dictate that the clubs that are going to succeed are Premier League clubs, and that actually it's a bit more thoughtful. I think we make more money than most other clubs because we have to make money, but we're not incentivised to make money. Most of the time we're just encouraged to go and ask for more money from the men's side. We can't do that.'

That expectation that a women's team would be dependent on the money generated by a men's team was almost ingrained in the narrative of women's football. The big occasions of the season were when the doors of the men's stadia were thrown open to the women – the Emirates, the Tottenham Hotspur Stadium, Stamford Bridge, Old Trafford – but there were other teams at the so-called smaller clubs, like Lewes, who played at the same ground as their male counterparts all year round. Murphy considered it almost an infatuation with top-flight men's football, and wished that fans and administrators could feel equally as fond of other aspects of the game.

'Can we be infatuated with the heart and the soul and the community?' she asked, going on to list the clubs that were doing things their own way in the Championship without getting any subsidies. 'It's very rare to get anything really unique [reporting] on Durham, who've done an amazing job with their women's set-up, or Coventry [United], who have done so much to get where they are, and now are slightly dismissed in a way. We're making more money than others, but we can't keep up [with the bigger clubs] even though we make more money. Is that fair, that we're trying to do this sustainably? I think this is an existential question for football.'

Legacy was something she thought about a lot, particularly in regard to the Lionesses' triumph a few months previously. What impact was it genuinely having week in, week out for Lewes?

'It's not really down to the FA, and it's not down to clubs,' she said. 'It's down to everyone that was excited or motivated. All the people that watched a game on TV or all the people who went to watch England or another country during the summer, how many of them have come back to go and see another game? I think the legacy is actually down to how much we've triggered individual people, not whether the FA has a legacy programme or whether a club is going to share more with their men's fan base. Did we push individuals over the line to go and support their local club?'

Her discussion of the licensing process indicated that Murphy and Lewes had a long-term plan stretching well into the future, but she refused to be drawn on her exact intentions for the next ten years.

'I don't know, and I still often think, "What would I do after this?" because it's super-stressful,' she said, before adding the unspoken fear: 'I don't know at what point Lewes might fail not because of us, but because of the ecosystem around us.'

* * *

'I never had an agent before,' said Lauren Heria. 'I signed with an agent a year ago, and she was like "Well, what clubs interest you? What about Championship clubs?" Straight away, I was like, "Honestly, Lewes is really the only Championship club – I would love to be there. I'd love to play with that club." A lot of it is because of how they present themselves and how they challenge things and how they want to make change. Football is football, but I feel that football has to be part of a bigger purpose.'

Heria, now 27 years old, had most recently played for London Bees, but had also represented Leyton Orient and Leicester United earlier in her career, having begun as a child at the Charlton Athletic girls' academy. Football was her life in many different ways, having achieved a Master's degree in sport business from Loughborough University in tandem with social media celebrity for her freestyle skills. That fame went some way to securing her a spot on the second series of *Ultimate Goal*, the reality TV series on BT Sport, where in 2021 female footballers got the chance to live and train like top professionals, with all the coaching and support network that suggests.

'My motivation for applying was it just seemed interesting! I thought it would give me a lot of things that I wanted in terms of trying to experience a little bit of what it's like to be a pro footballer. At the time, I was doing quite a lot of TikTok, so I was like, "It's not going to harm me to go on TV." It intrigued me more than anything. So I applied, went on it, and it was cool. The girls were really nice, and it really opened my eyes: there was so much talent, all of us were near enough tier four [two divisions below the Championship]. Mia Parry, for example, amazing player, she ended up then going and signing for Blackburn. There were some young players that are now in the Watford set-up. It just highlighted to me how much talent there is out there that's just unknown, basically. "How are you not playing higher? You're so talented."'

Heria had spent much of her playing career prior to this series in tiers three and four, and had come to the conclusion that the raw talent on offer might not have been too much different to that at a higher level; it was the coaching that really turned decent players into good ones.

'[At a lower level] you might get one training session, two training sessions a week. The standard of the coaching isn't as good as you get at your Championship clubs. So if these girls have had the ability to progress to this level, through this system, if you put them in a Championship club, what could they do?'

Spending two weeks in a competitive environment, with television cameras capturing this out-of-the-ordinary experience, might sound stressful, but Heria had very fond memories of it.

'The girls were awesome, and I'm still in contact with quite a few of them. In terms of filming, it was really challenging. I think I found it quite personally challenging because it was the first time I was away from home since my mum passed away. I had been very much at home, we'd gone through Covid [and lockdown], all of this, so to then go into that environment was quite intense.'

Heria had plenty of praise for the programme's celebrity coaches, former England stars Eniola Aluko and Rachel Brown-Finnis plus twins Rosie and Mollie Kmita, who she thought always had the players' best interests at heart. Sometimes the rigours of producing a television show did begin to tell: having to do retakes for particular shots, for example, or having a camera in one's face after a bad training session. Rather amusingly, none of the players got to watch the series back live as it aired; all of them who were still in England found that their club training sessions clashed with its broadcast time, and those who went overseas did not have access to it. When Heria saw it, though, she enjoyed it.

'They filmed pretty much every waking second for two weeks, and then in the edit I don't think they'd done anything to make people look bad or whatever. I think it was really true, the way they edited [it]. I was really happy with it, I think it played it out pretty true to how I was. It was nice, it was cool to see back – just something very unique.'

One year later, Heria and her women's sport consultancy Equal Kicks were involved in the Euros, providing expertise for security and logistics planning. It was the first contract her company had secured since she completed her postgraduate study.

'For me as a footballer it was a super-interesting experience. I got a lot of understanding of how the teams moved, in terms of how they were training and what equipment they needed; obviously as an athlete to see that at the highest level of football and be able to understand that was just incredible. Did I take away a lot to then bring back and implement in my training? Maybe not, but I think the big thing I took away was to just understand the athletes' professionalism, the staff's professionalism, how everything is so, so spot on and so purposeful and how they move and what they do and it was incredible.'

Three weeks after the Euros Final, Heria signed for Lewes. She knew plenty about the club, with her analysis of their operation forming part of her dissertation, and was sure they would be a perfect fit for her.

'Women and girls still face barriers, particularly women and girls from ethnic minorities,' she said. 'We still need to fight, we still need to make change, and Lewes has that focus: we want to create great football, we want you to play great football, and when we're on the training pitch, we are very much focused on the football and on the playing pitch we're focused on the football, but then you're part of that wider ecosystem that's actually trying to make a change. So yeah, it is a really perfect fit.'

Heria was never worried about speaking her mind publicly because she knew her values aligned with the club's, and she admired people like Maggie Murphy who were working so hard to create a different kind of football club and yet were still happy to spare time to share their thoughts and knowledge. That kind of expertise was also helping Heria as she continued to build her consultancy, although she refused to say she was looking ahead to her career after retirement on the pitch.

'I'd like to say I'm in my prime,' she said.

She had struggled with her mental health throughout her life, and wondered if she would have done better had she had more support from the football teams she played for as a child and as an adolescent. Certainly had she had the opportunity to stay in football via a talent pathway and perhaps had the chance to play at the highest level while pursuing her education, as girls ten years younger have been able to do, she thought her footballing career might have taken off much sooner.

'There are girls I played with in the [Charlton] academy, like Kit Graham, Molly Bartrip, Fliss Gibbons, they've gone on to play WSL, so it was possible, but for me it didn't work out. My journey through football has been very different, very sporadic, but I love playing and you get one life, so I need to try now to do what I can do now. I definitely have ambitions to go abroad and play as well. It's something I want to do, live abroad and experience different cultures, and football could be a great way to do that still. I'm just going to give it everything I've got until I can't anymore.'

Stepping up to tier two in the latter stages of her playing career meant she was perhaps not getting quite as many minutes on the pitch as she might have hoped for, but she was happy with her choices and with her progress.

'I'm not having the impact on the pitch that I had at Bees or at Orient, but I can see the strengths I bring,' she said. 'Everything I've done off the field I bring in some way to the field, like my leadership, my teamwork. We've got players who are 21 and doing their dissertations – great, I can sit down and help with that, I can do all that stuff!

'That's another nice thing about women's football: that collection of experiences and journeys and different sorts of players, types of people, that make a team successful. For me, Lewes epitomises that, because player for player, should we be going out and beating Crystal Palace? I don't know, but we are going out and beating Crystal Palace, beating Charlton, beating clubs with bigger budgets than us. A lot of that comes from what we've created and the team we've created and the atmosphere, so yeah. I'll keep playing football until I can't, basically.'

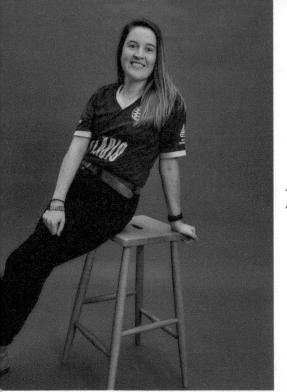

Helen Hardy, founder of Manchester Laces

Jo McDonald of Manchester Laces

Yasmine Elgabry of Manchester Laces

Shrewsbury Town Women captain Vikki Owen in action during the FA Cup match against Wolverhampton Wanderers

Shrewsbury Town Women's Maddie Jones (7) celebrates her goal against Wolves

Jo Butler-Williams in action for London Seaward [TouchTightmedia]

London Seaward
captain Giorgia Bracelli
[TouchTightmedia]

Liam Gilbert, manager of
Oxford United Women
[Darrell Fisher]

Shelly Provan of Oxford United Women [Darrell Fisher]

Jenna Legg of Oxford United Women [Darrell Fisher]

Lauren Heria on signing for Lewes [Lewes FC]

Maggie Murphy, CEO of Lewes FC [Lewes FC]

Stef McLoughlin, Lewes FC's commercial manager

England's Lionesses celebrate winning the Women's Finalissima in April 2023

6

Link

FOR ANYONE not interested in football – or who wanted to avoid watching the World Cup in Qatar – ITV's annual big-name celebrity reality TV offering hit the small screens. It did, however, feature one of the summer's triumphant Lionesses, Jill Scott, striding into camp via a skyscraper plank-walking challenge in which she summoned impressive nerves of steel and encouraged campmates Babatunde Aléshé and Charlene White to do the same. By the end of November, she was crowned Queen of the Jungle, with fiancée Shelley Unitt by her side.

A few weeks after Scott's reality television triumph, her fellow Lioness Beth Mead achieved another accolade – the coveted BBC Sports Personality of the Year award in recognition of her goalscoring feats for England in the summer. It was handed to her on the Wednesday before Christmas, when her Arsenal team-mates were in Zurich for a UEFA Women's Champions League match.

Mead was not there because she had ruptured her anterior cruciate ligament against Manchester United in the Women's Super League at the end of November. Three weeks after that, her team-mate and partner Vivianne Miedema suffered the same injury in a Champions League match against Lyon. The social media photos of the pair on crutches were heartbreaking. Miedema's post confirming her diagnosis endeavoured to bring some levity to a sad situation: 'At least we've still got two decent ACLs between us,' she wrote, adding: 'Can't wait to do some boxing in the gym after she's been annoying me for a while.'

But Miedema's observation, 'Sadly enough it's part of football,' was both shocking and a little sickening. These two superstars joined the likes of Spain's Ballon d'Or winner Alexia Putellas and France goal machine Marie-Antoinette Katoto on crutches and on the sidelines. The frequency of these injuries in the women's game is a huge concern, particularly as the exact reasons for it happening are under-researched. Although these were high-profile cases, the same thing is and has been happening at all levels of the women's game for many, many years.

'I was playing American football at school in PE, and I went to receive the ball, and it went – like, everyone heard it pop, and I was like, "Oh, this is weird,"' recalled Yasmine Elgabry. 'I tried to stand up, and fell straight back down, and also [it's] quite embarrassing when you're at school and that happens, because you can't cry, so … yeah. So that happened.'

Elgabry was 17 when she tore her anterior cruciate ligament. Born and brought up in the United States, where girls playing football is entirely routine, she had started kicking a ball when she was two and a half. Developing into a good goalkeeper, she joined a competitive club as a teenager, and intended to fund her tertiary education via a soccer scholarship; strong players are sought out by American colleges, keen to have them on their teams.

'I never wanted to become a professional footballer, but I've always wanted to play competitively,' she explained. 'I anticipated that my family couldn't afford to pay to send me to uni so I thought that would be my meal ticket in, and I could go to uni, study what I wanted, but have this as a way to get me through it and do something that I enjoy.'

She knew as soon as her knee popped that it was an ACL injury and that her plans were smashed to pieces.

'The second it happened, I realised, well, it's not happening because I'd spend my key year of being scouted in rehab,' she said. 'I had to leave the club I was playing for – right before a European tournament, so I missed out [on] a lot of things at that time in my life were the most important things to exist ... one year [in rehab away from playing] when you're a teenager, those things are the end of the world, and you have to entirely reconsider everything, so I had to pull through and get my grades to get me through uni.'

Time had, of course, given Elgabry perspective. 'Now if I heard about a 17-year-old going through this, I'm like, "Oh, my God, that's such a hard decision to make," and how it all alters everything you planned for. It prepares you to be resilient and those sorts of things, which are all really important things to happen in your teenage years, in your formative years.'

Elgabry had surgery on her knee almost immediately, just over a month after the injury, but the operation necessitated a lengthy recovery period. The longer she stayed away from the pitch, the more anxious she was about ever putting her boots back on again. Instead, she tried out some other sports that were considered less likely to incur wear and tear on her knees, and ended up tearing her meniscus at the age of 20, meaning more surgery.

'I found it a lot harder to recover from: I don't know if it was being 17 to being 20, I don't know what it was, but it was a lot harder,' she said, 'and I just figured I wouldn't be able to play again.'

She moved to England for postgraduate study at Manchester University in 2014, and met her future husband. They settled in the city, buying a house and even homing a cat, and Elgabry began to progress in her career. It was a colleague's passing remark that made her think of taking up football again.

'I was just mentioning like, "Oh, I hurt my knee, I played football for years and had to stop," and she's like, "Oh, I play on a football team … you should come along,"' she recalled. 'When I tell you the anxiety I had, because it had just been so long – so, so long! – and I was so out of shape and so scared. It was like, "I'm not going to be able to run a lap on the field, it's going to be embarrassing and horrible!"'

It was neither embarrassing nor horrible. Elgabry enjoyed that first session and found her knees were absolutely able to cope. She wondered later whether her fretting had built up a mental block and kept her away from football, even though she had thought repeatedly about going back.

'I probably thought [about football] a lot, and just had the urge – "I'll just have a kickabout!" – but it's not as fun when you're by yourself. There's something about playing with a team and being competitive, and being a goalkeeper, I like the adrenaline and I like all that stuff that comes with it.'

Nevertheless, she was glad that she had returned, even after more than a decade away.

'When you move to a new country as an adult, it's very hard to make friends, and I think the social aspect of football has been really invaluable to me,' she said. 'It is just so nice to be able to meet people and there's automatically something you have in common, right? Even if you have nothing else, you have this.'

With her new club, called Manchester Laces, she played in a competitive nine-a-side team – a reduced number of players that she did not think she would enjoy, but found herself appreciating, particularly with the smaller goal. She made sure she did plenty of strength work and stretches to ensure her knees and surrounding muscles were coping well with the load.

'For the most part, I don't feel too anxious about [my knees],' she said. 'The hardest bit is because I don't have tissue or meniscus or anything in one of my knees, so I have osteoarthritis. I knew it was going to happen so I find this time of year can be a little bit harder to play just because everything's stiff – I feel like someone's gran going out there! But I know how to take care of these things now which I guess is the most important thing, and I know when to stop, and I know when it's OK.'

After surgeries on both knees, Elgabry knew that she may never be the player she thought she might have become when she was a teenager, but she was happy with her life and her football, especially with finding a club that understood her limitations and her requirements.

'I just thought, "You know what, if I can find a team I can play for, where I'm not playing to play professionally, but I can play to how I feel, and some weeks my knees might not be as good as others, then I'll do it," so here I am – 15 years later.'

* * *

Manchester Laces was a very special football club, and if founder Helen Hardy – born in Newcastle, and newly relocated to the north-west after spending time in London – had known a few more people in the city when she had moved there with her wife, it might never have existed at all.

Hackney Laces had been the first team with that suffix, set up in 2011 and boasting a proudly inclusive ethos, working on social projects within the community and promoting opportunities for girls and women. It was the brainchild of player and coach Katee Hui, who went on to play for South London Laces, the offshoot team Hardy joined when she was in the capital.

'The work they do is absolutely incredible in Hackney,' enthused Hardy. In Manchester, though, as she looked to settle in and make new friends, she could not find a grassroots club with a similar set of principles – one that welcomed everyone, no matter her playing standard. If Hardy was going to continue playing and meet people through football, it looked like she would have to do it herself. She set up a call with the Laces committee to ask for their advice, and soon realised that setting up a club is much more difficult than she or anyone could ever have imagined.

'I know it seems so silly but pulling 16 kits together is actually really expensive and difficult and costs thousands of pounds,' she explained. 'Then having a club logo and having a website and deciding on a name: it's all like a little bit of time because you have to have something behind that name, there has to be meaning behind it.'

Hui and the rest of the Laces committee had no doubt: they wanted Hardy to take on the name and become part of the Laces family, carrying on the brand's work in Manchester.

'That was a no-brainer for me, because I am a Laces player, always have been,' said Hardy, adding with a smile: 'And in the administrative sense, this really saves me a task, having to come up with the concept! It just felt like a really easy and exciting step to take.'

Hackney Laces helped Hardy sort out the Manchester kit – the same design as the London Laces teams – and colour, opting for a honey yellow as the main shade as a nod to the city's famous bee symbol.

'The rest, as they say, is history,' said Hardy. However, that was where most of the hard work for her personally truly began.

With two friends who were also looking for a new club to join, Hardy picked a date for the launch of Manchester Laces, which she looked back on as 'anxiety-inducing'. They set up accounts across social media announcing the first-ever training session, sharing it across their networks and hoping for more traction. They did, however, have one major obstacle to overcome.

'We didn't have a venue!' admitted Hardy. 'So this whole time people were going, 'I might give this a go! Are you in north Manchester?' and I was like, 'Bear with me on that one!'

'We realised very quickly that there is a huge accessibility issue in women's football in particular and what that came from was the legacy problem. Men's football teams had been in those [football training] venues for 15 years, and so we were going to venues and they were saying, "Sorry, we're full up, men's clubs are already here, they've been here 15 years, they've paid us every month so we're not going to kick them out, are we?"'

Hardy was frustrated and furious. Women's football for leisure was a relatively new development, and that could not be detached from the impact of the 1921 decision to prevent women from playing football on FA-affiliated pitches; the ban lasted half a century and even after that, societal attitudes were still slow to change. The idea that girls should not and did not play football continued to fester, stunting the footballing growth of generations of girls, and still hampering them into adulthood.

'It wasn't like there were regular amateur teams that you could go to 15 years ago. They were few and far between, so we weren't able to take that space,' continued Hardy. 'It's not fair – I would be a legacy club for you, one that was paying every month, if we'd even known we could play football 15 years ago.'

Hardy and the fledgling Manchester Laces struck gold when a south Manchester venue, Whalley Range, reopened after refurbishing its astroturf provision. The centre manager was a big fan of women's football and admired the work Hackney Laces had done in London, and rang Hardy at 7pm one Friday night, full of excitement and enthusiasm, to offer her that space. Pleased as Hardy was to finally have a venue confirmed, she was a little taken aback by the positivity.

'I was thinking, "Oh, wait, we're nothing, we've done nothing – I think that you're thinking we are Hackney Laces, but it's just me and my two mates – but OK, let's roll with this!"' she said. With the pitches booked and a supportive venue, Hardy was now even more driven to make sure the space was full. She ran an online retailer dedicated to women's football, so felt that she had a little bit of an advantage when it came to targeting those who might be interested in kicking a ball themselves. That was only a small part of her strategy, though.

'The big thing was our unique differentiator, which was that we wanted to be inclusive to everybody, and we wanted to move our goalposts around our players,' she explained. 'So what that meant to me was individually messaging people with bespoke responses. People would be like, "I'm really nervous because I've never played football before," and I would say, "I promise you're not alone, you will not be alone, I will be there. Here's a photo of me, this is what I look like, I'm going to meet you in the car park."'

Ensuring that everyone who expressed an interest got a response, and a personalised one at that, was key for Hardy, who had often found other amateur clubs rather unwelcoming at first contact. A brief exchange of initial emails would just result in a potential new player being given only the basic details she would require to get to training – nothing that would make her feel reassured or wanted.

'I'm a confident person but I don't know how I'd feel about going to a dark venue at eight o'clock at night in December – this is really terrifying,' explained Hardy. 'Now imagine you're trans, non-binary, entering a space where you're already struggling to leave the house because you feel so nervous about how you're going to be perceived and what the world thinks of you – and then somebody is like, "Meet me at eight o'clock in the dark car park!" It's just not going to happen, it's just not feasible.'

Hardy's insistence on a personalised, humanised approach was reflected in the club's website too. With slight tweaks to the existing Hackney Laces design assets, the Manchester Laces online presence already looked very professional; then Hardy and her two co-founders put their names and faces on the site's welcome page. Anyone casually browsing and considering giving football a go would already know who to look out for when they got to the venue.

They launched in March 2021, just as the pandemic-enforced lockdowns began to lift again.

'Football isn't necessarily about going out and winning loads of 11-a-side games and trying to get to the top of football, it's also about community and coming together and empowering each other and making friends and meeting loved ones, and all of that stuff that comes with being part of something epic,' said Hardy. 'I remember session one; there was about 50 people that came along on that first night, and I thought, "Whoa, I thought we were going to pull together an 11-a-side team, but actually I think this is a service that people really need and people really want." What I realised very quickly was – and this was even before the amazing work of the Lionesses with the Euros – people were starting to feel more empowered to try football for the first time as adults. They were seeing, "This is a space that maybe I can enter into," when they had never really felt like that before.

'We found that around 60% of the people that came that night had never kicked a ball before and then the rest were kind of like five-a-side players or had been more casual or maybe had just left their team during Covid and wanted to try out a new vibe or energy so had come to try our club – and we've just grown from there.'

After less than two years in existence, Manchester Laces were massively successful, and still expanding. They offered ad hoc sessions, with players unable to commit to every week and paying when they were able to attend, and membership sessions, always building on the previous week's progress and giving players the chance to develop. Training for members was split into five squads, from beginners up to competitive amateur 11-a-side football, encompassing around 160 players, with more than 550 people attached to the club as part of the wider network.

'Those five squads represent, I would say, just about everyone in Manchester,' reflected Hardy. 'It's just a real vibrant group of people across all five squads and you could slot everybody from every walk of life into those groups depending on their ability level and their football journey.'

Importantly, the club was led by women and non-binary individuals, with female and non-binary coaches, even though Hardy was quick to note that the lack of men was not necessarily intentional. Many of the players wanted to be coached only by a female, whether that was for cultural or other reasons, but others would welcome a male coach should he be appointed. However, by the end of 2022, the Manchester Laces' leadership positions were all filled by women and non-binary people.

'I'm really proud of that,' admitted Hardy. She said that the club refused to settle for second-best and simply appoint anyone who expressed any interest in working with them. 'I think there can become a bit of a desperation when you're growing at the speed that we are to just settle and be like, "We need a coach, level one, come on in!"

'But we do have a real process with coaches, when we bring them in, about being really clear about our ethos. Before anything, before we'd done night one with 50 people coming along, we wrote a 15-page ethos around what we stood for and what meant something to us.'

Whenever a coach applied to work with Manchester Laces, they would receive that document, and their response – or otherwise – told Hardy and the rest of the committee everything they needed to know.

'Often you just didn't hear back from coaches if they didn't stand by that [document]. From a personal perspective, we play in leagues now, and you go up against opposition, and sometimes it's not necessarily the words that the [opposition] coaches are saying to their players, sometimes it's really positive, it's the tone. After 18 months of being around positive affirmation constantly, it's really triggering when you hear a coach being like, "Come *on*, you can do it, man!" and you're like, "Oh, I just forgot what it was like to have that type of coaching."

'We just don't have that culture within our club, it just doesn't exist. I can't put my finger on how, but I guess if you buy into the culture and ethos, you're likely to not be the sort of person that is a coach that will be aggressive in your demeanour. [We see opposition teams where] at half-time all the women [players] sit on the floor and the man [coach] stands above them and will be pointing around the group. In our circle, we go in and once we've got our arms around each other, then our coach Claire will say, "Who wants to go first?" and then it will be an open forum for discussion. We never raise our voices with each other and it's just really kind and empowering. We could be losing 4-0 – and we usually are – and it just doesn't seem to matter.'

With so many people enthusiastically buying into Hardy's vision for an inclusive, friendly, grassroots football club, Manchester Laces had already progressed far beyond what she could ever have imagined.

'I was just looking for a few friends,' she said, 'and then I got 500 of them.'

It was not just the club members who had noticed and appreciated Hardy's work and the boom in growth for the Manchester Laces. The city was home to the National Football Museum, who wanted to be sure they captured for posterity the work the club was doing, and took for display the honey-themed home kit plus their newly designed away kit, based on the Pride flag and the colours of the LGBTQ+ communities. Hardy was also interviewed for a museum project, featuring alongside the likes of Chelsea manager Emma Hayes and Arsenal midfielder Kim Little. In fact, her personal profile was beginning to rise as several organisations highlighted and praised her individual contributions to grassroots women's football. The National Lottery selected her as one of the faces of a new campaign, representing sport in the local community, which resulted in a rather surprising honour – the announcement that her face would be projected on to Wembley Stadium, with Lionesses captain Leah Williamson the one to switch the light on.

'I don't really understand, I keep thinking it might be a joke,' confessed Hardy. 'They came into my office, they took some photographs of me and then off they went into the world. The next thing, Leah Williamson messaged me and said, "Hey, we're meeting up [at the event in December] and it would be cool to catch up before then to chat about it!" My mum and dad are beside themselves with excitement.'

That did not mean that Hardy and Manchester Laces were content to simply continue with what they were doing. They were already looking for new ways to offer football to as much of the community as they could possibly manage. With five squads, they were already operating near to their existing capacity, and so Hardy was considering ways to expand further.

'What I'd love to do – and I've been speaking to the Manchester United Foundation about it – is introducing [coaching for] the level below adult women, so that would be [ages] 13 to 16,' she said. 'I think there is a huge gap there for young girls and teenagers who want to access football for the first time.'

She pointed to the popularity of football with little girls, who lost their place to play after they were no longer allowed to compete in the same team as their male peers, and the need to encourage teenagers back into sport and fitness; she wondered if there was the possibility for Manchester Laces to offer the same range of coaching for teenage girls as they already did for adult women, from a casual kickaround to a competitive 11-a-side set-up.

At the other end of the scale, she hoped to offer walking football for older women, and had already spoken to Manchester City's community department about a potential collaboration.

'It's something I'm super-passionate about,' she said. 'We already have quite a lot of players who are in their fifties and sixties who are like, "I love Manchester Laces but I'm just not sure how much longer my football career is going to last."

'Where we are right now is we've got this massive adult club that benefits people from age 16 to realistically 65, 66 years old. What can we look at either side of that? Then within that as well, what more can we offer to more areas of the community? Never shut our doors – that's my goal.'

* * *

Jo McDonald, in her fifties, was not one of Manchester Laces' oldest players, but she was certainly on the more senior end of the spectrum. She loved football as a child, but found her interest crushed by school rules. Though she would kick a ball around with her friends in the street after school, there was no chance of her playing in an organised team.

'When I stopped playing out in the street when I was a teenager that was it, I didn't play again,' she said. 'All I saw was the men's game. At school we were told girls can't play football and you just accepted it in those days – you were scared of the teachers, it was that sort of environment. We had separate playgrounds at primary school, the boys and the girls, they weren't allowed to have balls in the girls' playground.'

Even at an all-girls' secondary school, there was no chance to play.

'I do remember mithering the PE teacher quite constantly to say, "Can we play football?" but again we weren't allowed to play. She used to say, "You know we can't, girls, you know we can't."'McDonald would not have described herself as a sporty person, although she always loved sport. ('I just wasn't very good at it!' she explained.) Big occasions like Wimbledon, the World Cup, or the Olympics would find her glued to the television, but not necessarily inspired to take up an activity herself. It was the effects of the rigours of lockdown that encouraged her to take action.

'I wanted to do some exercise but I don't like the gym. My daughter moved to London and she said she'd found this exercise class where they do running about and they kick a ball and it's fun and it's social, and she said, "I thought you might like it if you found something somewhere near you where they do something like that." I didn't expect it to be a football team. I thought it would be drills, a little bit of a fun ten-minute game at the end maybe, but just running and being active and being outdoors.'

112

McDonald spotted the Manchester Laces posts on social media, and thought she was walking into some sort of football fitness class, and was more than a bit taken aback by what she described as the 'full-on' nature of the first-ever session.

'I'd searched over the years for women's teams and not really come across anything that was close by or that I was able to get to,' she explained. 'When I looked for "exercise classes with football", it came up on my Instagram for the first session of Laces and that's how I found it. I just thought, "You know what, after lockdown I'm just going to give it a go, I'm going to try it. What's the worst that can happen? If I don't enjoy it, I come home, and I never see them again." That's what I did.'

She was intimidated not just by the other players' youth but their fitness levels, and found herself collapsing in a hot, exhausted heap at the end.

'I said, "I don't think I can do this," and [the coach] said, "Please come again next week because you'll be surprised how quick your fitness comes, and you obviously love it" – because I did. As soon as I started kicking the ball, I just loved it, kicking it, the joy that I had as a child was suddenly there again. So, yeah, I thought, "I'll come along and try and give it a go again," and after the second session that was it, I was pretty much obsessed with coming along. It was just pure joy, I had so much joy doing it, so that was it.'

One might have expected McDonald's daughter to be rather pleased with the success of her suggestion – but that has not been the case.

'She doesn't remember actually saying it!' laughed McDonald. In fact, her daughter only went to her own football fitness session once, just before the lockdowns started, and after that she moved house and wasn't able to go again.

And coach Candice's post-session positive comment was a big factor in encouraging McDonald to go back. It would not be an exaggeration to say that being part of Laces had changed her life, not just improving her fitness but her social life, and finally giving her the football community she had wanted since she was a little girl.

'I never imagined going to that first session that I would enjoy it so much,' she said. 'I just thought it'll be a bit of fun, a bit of exercise, it'll get me outdoors, I might meet some people – after lockdown, I was ready to meet people and chat. I'm much fitter now because I play football three times a week and I met loads of people that I probably would never have come across in my life – loads of young people as well, they keep me young.

'The other chance encounter was Candice actually taking the time to speak to me after the session and saying, "Please come again," because after that first session I thought I'd give it a go, and I enjoyed it but I couldn't actually do it, I was not physically capable of doing it. If she hadn't have said, "Come again and try again and your fitness will come," if she hadn't had that belief and support, I don't think I would have gone again for the second time. I'm glad she did.'

McDonald's delight in her new-found football club was palpable. It was not just about the way it had positively affected her own life, but how much she loved being part of a squad. After so many years of asking to play football and being rejected, she finally had her home.

'I didn't run before – I couldn't run – but it's mad that once you're with your team-mates you want to work for each other, and just have fun,' she said.

'It's just a ball, and it's for everybody. It really is for everybody: no matter who you are, how much money you've got. You can play it anywhere around the world, and it is the simplest game.'

* * *

Sapphire Brewer-Marchant, an actor, had joined Manchester Laces as a welcoming, inclusive space. They had found that the city felt like a true home after starting to understand themselves as non-binary.

'I'd never really entertained the idea of living in Manchester because in my head it was always London [where I wanted to be]: I guess that's the actor in me, like I have to be in London,' they explained. 'But yeah, I did a show up in Manchester, saw a lot of Manchester, and was like, "Actually, I could live here," and then I looked at prices, and compared them with London, and was like, "Yeah, I'm definitely moving to Manchester!"'

Brewer-Marchant had grown up on the island of Guernsey, and been an excellent young footballer. From the age of nine, they played in teams alongside their male peers; when they turned 11, they were not allowed to play with the boys anymore. It took them a while to find a training option in the relatively small community, but when they did, they were soon part of the island's representative team.

'I was actually the first girl in my football team to be included in the A-team, which was a massive thing, and I had a lot of support from the boys, but then as time went on, the more I played, the less respect I felt like I had from them,' they recalled. 'There were specific women's teams, but you could only be 15 onwards or 16 onwards in order to play with them, so I had a few years where I wasn't really doing much because I couldn't play with the boys.

'I did try to go back when I was 14, because then I was allowed to [when the rules were adjusted] and I just remember walking into that first training session with my old team and some people that I used to play with, and I just heard, "Why is a girl here?" and I never went back.'

Brewer-Marchant left Guernsey when they were 18 to pursue their acting career, moving to London for drama school, and never finding a football team to settle with. They returned to Guernsey during the pandemic, then spent time with an aunt in York where they began to make the first steps into realising their non-binary identity. They had felt like an outsider at the clubs they had tried out in adulthood, but the success of the Lionesses in Euro 2022 encouraged them to give it another go.

'I basically Googled "non-binary-friendly football groups in Manchester", because at the time I had just recently come out as non-binary and I wasn't sure if I was ever going to be able to play football,' they said. 'Manchester Laces were the first team that came up so I just emailed them and then was met with a lovely response. I joined in August [2022] and have been loving it ever since.'

As Brewer-Marchant continued on their progress of understanding themselves better, they found huge support from their new team-mates.

'The first session I went there, I fitted in straight away,' they said. 'Everyone was gendering me correctly; introductions are always names and pronouns, which I have never experienced ever before, so it was just amazing.

'Recently I was in Guernsey doing *Hamlet* and I came up with a new kind of nickname for me, 'Fire', because it was 'Saff' before, but I felt like that was just a bit too feminine. So 'Fire' came about in Guernsey, and I messaged the group chat just before I came back – "Hey, I've been trying out 'Fire' as a nickname, feel free to use it if you want, either that or Sapphire is fine," and literally the first session back, everyone was calling me "Fire" and it was just incredible.'

Brewer-Marchant also loved the content of the Laces training sessions, including fitness work as well as skill. Their enthusiasm for the club, and regained love of the match, was evident in every word they spoke.

'Growing up, I always felt like I had to prove that I was a good footballer, so I always used to get so much anxiety when I had to play football, especially if I knew people were going to be watching,' they said. 'I was like, "I have to prove that I am good enough to be doing this," whereas I didn't even feel that on my way to my first training session for Laces which is something that I've never experienced before.

'Even before stepping into the safe space that Laces have created, I was already feeling safe enough to not have to feel like I had to prove myself, and I think that's a testament to Laces and what they're trying to achieve.'

7

Community

LONDON SEAWARD were using the gap in the men's fixture calendar to raise awareness of their club in the local community. With funding from the local council, they put on an event in the community, staffed by players volunteering their spare time, and found that although people were aware of the football ground in Walthamstow, many had no idea there was a tier four women's club playing there. Lots of small children came along, much to the club's surprise, as they were expecting more older children and teenagers.

'It was good to get our name out there, and it was very heart-warming, a lot of young kids having a good time, little boys, little girls,' said captain Giorgia Bracelli, who acknowledged that there was also a touch of frustration there with the public's general lack of knowledge of Seaward's existence; perhaps after the summer there had been hopes that women's football would suddenly boom at all levels.

'The good thing is that it is so easy that once you get them [the children] engaged,' she added. 'The atmosphere around it [women's football] is so positive – like when we've had mascots down, they've come again, because the kids love it. They wouldn't be able to walk out with a tier four men's club as easily as they do for us. Then the second time, once people are at the game, it's fun, the experience is positive. The issue is getting people there.'

Bracelli also thought that the day in the community reached a demographic they might not have expected: many were young women, some now with children of their own, who told the players how much they wished they had had the opportunity to play football themselves when they were younger.

'There is a lack of knowledge more than anything else,' concluded Bracelli, 'and once you get past that barrier, you get to engage people a lot more easily.'

'Most people now know the WSL and Championship, but even four or five years ago, I probably wouldn't have been able to tell you what the top tiers in the women's game were called,' admitted Jo Butler-Williams, who after her work with Seaward had just accepted a job with the FA. 'It's about awareness. At the end of a game, if we don't sell some programmes that were printed, we'll just take them to the pub and we'll put them on a table and people want to know who we are. Getting ourselves out there is so important, just that exposure, because people want to engage. It's just they actually don't know we exist, which is hard.'

Butler-Williams and the rest of the Seaward committee were focused on bringing in more volunteers to help improve the matchday experience for fans coming through the turnstiles.

'If you can make sure that someone's on the gate every week, if you can make sure that there's someone on the tannoy, that there's someone tweeting, doing those little things, it really does help drive things along because the more people can get involved with it, the easier it gets,' she said.

'That balance of volunteers and players and getting people engaged; it's a real tricky thing for our league and the league above,' added Bracelli. 'We're in a transition phase at the moment. Some clubs are getting professionalised, and some clubs are much closer to grassroots. So the players who come in, you want them to feel really engaged with the club, and to volunteer and feel like they're part of the [club's] identity. But you also want to give them the experience of a tier four club, where the standards are high on the football pitch as well.

'It's a very interesting time to be a part of that because players are here for different reasons, and the challenge you might have sometimes is some players might want to come to play football and that isn't necessarily wrong, but you also want them to buy into it and to get involved with the club because we don't have the resources that maybe some of the other big clubs do. So it will be interesting to see what happens in the next few years in our league because I think it will just get more and more professionalised, which is really good, but on the flip side, there's lots of smaller clubs that might find it more difficult. Hopefully that's not us.'

Butler-Williams and her colleagues on the committee had said earlier in the season that a good run in the Women's FA Cup was invaluable to a club like Seaward, bringing in a significant chunk of income since the prize money pot had been extended. They reached the second round proper – a huge achievement for a club of their size and support.

'Our bank balance is definitely a lot more comfortable than it was,' agreed Butler-Williams. 'We're now thinking two, three years [ahead], not two, three minutes. We were very much at a point where we weren't able to think strategically, we weren't able to make those kinds of investments that pay off later, whereas now we're thinking, "OK, what is it that we can invest in now?" Even just simple things: like if you can get a sponsor for three years, then you buy that kit for three years, it's not buying a kit for a season. All of those little things can really start to pay back to your club.

'The FA Cup winnings, I haven't heard a single team that didn't go, "It's just brilliant that it has changed like that." It is non-comparable. Before, it wasn't even worth writing it into your budget. Now, obviously we don't count on that [prize money], but it has now given us a complete buffer for next season. That's such a huge thing for us to be able to now do that.'

They were a little reticent to admit it, but both Butler-Williams and Bracelli thought that the monetary value put on cup matches gave them an extra incentive to play well. The Seaward players were well aware of the way the club operated, and the difference just a few hundred pounds could make.

'People aren't expecting the world but they're grateful for what we can give, and also have bought into it,' explained Bracelli. 'We've had really good take-up on individual player sponsors, for example [because we have] been honest about how much that kind of money makes a difference.

'I think all [our] players have an understanding of how much it costs to rent a football pitch or [buy] that kit or why they're getting that kit in that situation and why the FA Cup winnings are important to us, which is really important for players to know because it's just good awareness, and then it makes you appreciate much more what work is done behind the scenes and being grateful for that.'

'Without my committee hat on and just thinking as a player,' added Butler-Williams, 'you literally feel five times more valuable than you did before.'

She also thought it made outsiders put more value on women's football. The Women's FA Cup game had even been an option on some betting sites, meaning that Butler-Williams could point to it in front of her friends and feel a sense that she was finally making them understand why she was so committed to football.

'It means more than just the value of the money given to the club,' she said. 'It changes people's impression of the game.'

* * *

Shrewsbury Town had not got beyond their Women's FA Cup first-round tie with Wolverhampton Wanderers. As their relative status in the game – two tiers apart – would have suggested to any casual onlooker, the higher-ranked team won by a substantial margin, defeating the Shrews 8-2 to progress to the next round.

Manager Tom Peevor was, however, not too disappointed.

'At that stage it was the toughest team we could have drawn so we were excited really because obviously Wolves

isn't too far away from us, and I am a Wolves fan actually!'
he said. 'It was a good one for us. We knew it was going to
be tough. We felt like we'd got a plan for them, and we were
just going to give them a good go, really.

'I thought that they would rotate a little bit and maybe
not play their strongest team but no, they played their
strongest team, they really went for it, which was great.
It showed a lot of respect for us, which I appreciate, to
be honest.'

Peevor's plan did work 'to a degree', he explained
with a grin.

'We did give them some problems! We nearly scored
in the first 30 seconds. I thought, "Please go in!" It didn't.
There we go.

'They have a certain way of playing, which we knew
about, but they're just so good at it. They're very quick,
athletic, have precision in what they do, and it was tough
for us because we're not used to playing a team that plays so
fast. So that's what probably undid us.'

Wolves had won their league the season before, but had
missed out on promotion after losing the regional play-off
final to Southampton. Peevor thought that Wolves were
essentially just a technically better team than his own, good
enough for the second tier; Shrewsbury, he thought, were
no less fit than their opponents had been, and he took care
to remember that his squad were all amateur players with
full-time jobs, many with responsibilities at home as well.
One was a mother with several children, and Peevor was
full of admiration for her commitment to her family and
her football.

'I'm amazed,' he said. 'I call her "supermum", because it's like, "How can she play, work, have those kids?" It's a lot to juggle. It's a unique situation [for a football coach], and I work hard to not forget that, because sometimes they have a long day at work, they might have had a really stressful day, and then they come to training at 8pm on a really cold night, which it is at the moment, cold, dark nights.

'And I think I can't be too demanding with them, because they've had a hell of a day. They've probably rushed home from work, had a little bit of food – probably didn't eat the food that they wanted to because they needed to be ready for training. Yeah, there's a few challenges before them along the way.'

He continued to rely on the support of his fellow coaches plus the staffing set-up at the foundation, which enabled him to offer his team not just good coaching on the pitch but any help and advice they needed off it as well, which he thought made Shrewsbury 'a little bit more advanced' than many of the other teams in the league. He was particularly grateful for the services of a media officer: 'In the early days it was me doing it and it was awful! [The social media graphic content] was WordArt. It was terrible!'

'There's been a massive change from five years ago,' agreed captain Vikki Owen. 'It was very separate. The women [had] their own identity, really. That went with our performance as well: we weren't as professional. Everything was just a little bit … not quite there. Our players were in it more for fun than to actually go out and win, whereas now we've got that really nice balance between all having fun, but we're all there for the same goal. All the coaching staff are amazing. We've got so much more support, and we're tied to the club now, on the social media, having sponsorships and all that kind of thing as well.'

Owen was one of the side's longer-serving players. As a child, she had started playing with a local team, but struggled to find too many clubs available to her when she progressed to senior football. She signed for Crewe Alexandra Ladies, playing for their development team, but ultimately wanted a club closer to her home in Wem, Shropshire, and that was when she joined Shrewsbury Town. Owen wanted to play at the highest possible level, but at the time she signed for the Shrews, the set-up was still firmly amateur, and unsurprisingly many of the better players gradually drifted away.

'We lost a lot of players,' she recalled. 'I started off just in the team and then I became vice-captain of the team. Then the captain left to go and play for another team and a lot of the players left at that point. So it was then, "Do I leave with everybody else or do I stay?" I knew where Shrewsbury could be as a club, obviously; it's a very well-known name. I knew where I wanted it to be and the potential of [the club].'

She gave Peevor much of the credit for helping to turn things around for the women's team, praising his vision for their progress, and showing the club what could be achieved in tandem with them.

'The season that the club were like, "Right, we're behind you, we're going to back you up, you're going to get sponsors" is the same season that we flipped everything around and won the league. The support came, and then we turned it all around. It was hand in hand.'

Owen knew that not all the teams in their league had quite the same approach as Shrewsbury, but thought the professionalism across all clubs was increasing as they progressed up the pyramid.

'You've got to control your controllables,' she smiled. 'When we went to training twice a week, at the beginning of last season, we were umming and aahing whether that was the right thing to do. I think Tom was a bit unsure whether we'd actually get people coming to train that often, just because of other commitments: everybody has full-time jobs and some have children and that kind of thing. It's difficult. It's a big commitment to give three times a week when you're already working full-time and have other responsibilities.

'As soon as we realised that we had quite a lot of numbers [at training] and it was very competitive, that made more people come. We were focused on ourselves, we knew where we wanted to be. Now we've gone up into the next league, I think we have stepped up with a little bit more professionalism as well in that sense in regards to the other teams in it: they've all got the same goal to progress and move forward as well.'

Owen loved being Shrewsbury's captain. She tried to strike a balance between friendliness and focus on football, and was pleased with the dynamic within the squad. She made sure she kept an eye on the younger players, and stayed in touch with everyone via messages away from matchday.

'I try to go above and beyond to do little things to make sure everybody knows that I'm thinking of them,' she said. 'We just had a Christmas party and I got everyone Christmas crackers and wrote everybody a card. I like to be that approachable captain, but also I want them to know that I'm here for business. I think I have the respect of everybody in the team but they also know outside of football hours I'm just friendly – as soon as I'm off the pitch I stop being bossy, I'm a nice person again!'

As Peevor had said, Owen and the rest of the team enjoyed the opportunity to go into the community and speak to little girls, some of whom were aspiring footballers themselves.

'Some of the older girls [in the team] didn't really have role models growing up, and there was no clear idea of, "Oh, that's who I want to be or where I want to aspire to be,"' she said, admitting that she had loved watching Kelly Smith and Rachel Yankey – forward players both, not much use for someone who became a defender. However, as a junior player she had had the chance to meet an up-and-coming young defender called Steph Houghton at a prize-giving ceremony. Houghton, of course, went on to captain England; although Owen and her team-mates might not have known who she was at the time, she was glad she had kept souvenirs of their meeting, including an autograph.

'When we occasionally get the chance to play in the actual men's stadium, and we get mascots coming down, like all the young local girls' teams, we stay after, we sign pictures for them. It's a very clear footpath on where they could be if they carry on with their football. It's not too out of their grasp to come and play for Shrewsbury Town when they're older if they wanted to, and I think that's really nice.'

She hoped that future generations of Shrewsbury Town players would be able to play at an even higher level.

'Teams are a bit faster, they are a bit tougher, but we've really gone up and held our own,' she pointed out. 'I think for us to go and win this league, even though we are the underdogs going into it, it is seeming to be something that we could actually achieve [one day].

'So [I'd like to see us] working up through the leagues but also as an older player now I really see my job as coaching the younger players, because we've got some really talented young players in our team that I think personally could go very far.

'I'm just trying to give them all of my knowledge and everything that I know so that they can grow up to go on and play football for whoever they want to, because they've got all that knowledge and experience, even though they're still very young.'

Owen was a student veterinary nurse, having bounced around from job to job in her younger years. She worked fixed hours, with weekends still free for football, but even so it was a big time commitment; with so much time spent on study, she had not thought too much about whether she might want to go into coaching more formally after the end of her playing career.

'I don't really have any coaching qualifications,' she said, 'but [I get coaching experience] just because I'm used to talking and captaining the teams. It wouldn't be something that I would be against going into, I think I would [like to] eventually when I finish, I would like to pass that experience on to other players, other teams, but it's just – where do I find the time to do that?'

She thought about it a little more.

'A lot of the men's footballers come out of football and go into coaching, don't they? Maybe that's something that we as a women's team need to look into. I think the club would be behind us, support us, if we wanted to do that; I'm sure they would help us get through our coaching badges. I'm sure that's something that Shrewsbury as a club would help us achieve if we wanted to get there.'

SPRING

8

Power

IT WAS starting to feel like winter was finally over. The clocks had not gone forward, so an early-evening walk through Manchester was still reliant on street lights illuminating the darkness. The long, straight road passed through the district with the city's tertiary education settings all clustered together, past the museum, past the hospital, into a busier, buzzier stretch packed with restaurants, clothes shops, jewellers and convenience stores. The frequent buses flew past in a procession, packed with passengers even before rush hour, depositing students away from their classrooms and back at their digs.

Turning right, the noisy road and bustling shops gave way to a quieter street. On one side, large houses were set back from the pavement behind high red walls. Further down the road were tall Victorian-style terraces, with the occasional window lit up as people returned home for the evening after a day at work. On the opposite side of the street was a pretty church, still with Christmas messages hanging outside, surrounded by a large park. The gates were open, and a group of men were working hard in a personal training session, with their instructor shouting commands to them. Cutting through the darkness were floodlights rising above the roofs, shining through the trees.

Platt Lane had once been an integral part of Manchester City's set-up, visible from their old Maine Road stadium, serving as their training ground and later the home of their youth teams. Since their relocation across the city to the vast Etihad complex – with its massive stadium for the men, and a smaller, neighbouring stadium for the women and the academy teams – Platt Lane had passed into county FA ownership, and then to Manchester Metropolitan University. Equipped with outdoor 3G pitches plus indoor space, the university housed its own sports teams there, and also opened up the doors to the local community.

This was where Manchester Laces trained on a Thursday evening. Like clockwork, as at so many other football facilities across the world, as the clock ticked towards the hour mark, one group headed off the turf as the next took their place, ready for the start of their allocated slot. The Laces were training on the full-size pitch furthest away from the entrance gate and the car park, and players walked quickly and carefully around the edge of the pitches preceding their own. Three of the Laces teams were training that night, and most of the players were already gathered ready to begin their warm-up at 6pm. Indeed, some already claimed to be warm, patting the turf as they pulled their boots on, with one declaring, 'This is toasty!' After the hours of training in the bitter cold, spring was surely on its way.

Platt Lane was not exactly tropical when it came to temperature. The tall, cage-like fence around the pitches led directly to the park, and offered little shelter from the elements. The Laces players donned and discarded extra layers according to their own requirements throughout; not for this club a regimented training kit. Instead, players wore whatever they were most comfortable in: a Manchester City replica shirt with Kevin de Bruyne's name emblazoned on the back, the deep blue national shirt of France, the dark red England away strip, a Ramones t-shirt, shorts, leggings, tracksuit bottoms. One shrugged off her snug puffa jacket to reveal a plaster cast on a broken left arm – no reason to miss football training.

Before the session began, some of the players started their own stretches and drills, with a couple taking advantage of the available equipment – a three-person free-standing wall, intended for free-kick practice. In the middle of a large group of female players, it was noticeable that the wall had most likely been designed for men; it was several inches taller than any of the free-kick takers or those standing in goal attempting to make a save. With few players seeming keen to take the gloves, there was an unspoken agreement to share the goalkeeping duties, everyone taking a turn, with some obviously more adept and more prepared for it than others.

The training drills led by coaches and senior players focused on encouraging technique with both feet, letting everyone have equal time on the ball, rather than going straight into a game. Indeed, with around 50 people on the pitch, organising a game that involved everyone would likely prove tricky. One of the groups enjoyed a series of relay races, with two teams competing against each other, and the 'losers' asked to do five star jumps as a forfeit. The laughter echoed around the complex.

On a pitch encircled only by a link cage fence, backing on to a public park, the passers-by were frequent. Most were dog walkers, their pets scampering into the shrubbery, or trotting obediently alongside their master or mistress. There was the occasional jogger, one lighting his own way with a head torch. One man decided to stop and watch and yell his own brand of encouragement to the players: 'Where is the passion?' he demanded of them. Getting no response from the group, he moved along relatively quickly.

The passion he demanded, though, was very much in evidence, had he cared to look rather than shout distracting and irritating clichés at a group of female footballers. The Laces teams featured players of all shapes and sizes, and across a wide age range. Jo McDonald, one of the most experienced players there, was also the most senior there that evening; as she grabbed two sacks of footballs plus a pack of orange bibs and stackable cones from the boot of her car before the session, she had enthused about the opportunity the Laces set-up offered even to complete beginners. As she later added, it was one thing attracting new players to the game in the height of summer in the first heady days of the aftermath of the Lionesses' triumph; it was quite another to keep them coming back every week as the temperatures dropped.

And Laces truly were bringing players back every week. This was only the Thursday training session, after all. They also had a drop-in session on a Monday, plus other teams training on a Wednesday, plus league competition on Wednesdays and Sundays, alongside the FA's new Flexi

League, which ran on different days throughout the season. An inclusive football club, offering training and matches for players of all abilities, might be an oddity in the men's game, with its participants expected to show 'passion' through tough tackles and raised voices. The Laces' players' passion, though, manifested itself through the supportive asides to each other, the smiles on the faces, the willingness to run a lap of the pitch to warm up by oneself after arriving late just to be part of the session. They played – as women through history have always done – for the love of their game, the game that McDonald kept describing as 'the simplest game in the world'.

* * *

Laces founder Helen Hardy had a theory about the man who had been shouting at the players through the fence. It was by no means the first time something like that had happened, and she thought there was an upsurge in such behaviour from men who felt demoralised and almost detached from football as more and more women took up the game instead. The fact that women's football was visibly, obviously popular as both a participation sport and a spectator sport was, she thought, even more troubling to such people.

'In the worst instance I think they have zero control over how they feel any more because there's nothing they can say or do that takes this away so it's just insults,' she said. She recalled an incident where a man stopped to shout abuse which she described as 'visceral'.

'I felt totally helpless in that moment,' she said, before adding that she thought there was little that could be done to change the minds of those men, nor those who refused to watch women's football even if they did not shout abuse at players in public. However, she did not think this was a problem specific to football, merely that football was a space in which these men's fear and dislike of women was being played out; and she thought there was a demographic of men who did not currently watch women's football but could still be won over.

'I think we're scaring people a lot with the power of the sport, which is an amazing sport,' she said. 'The best facet of the sport – which I think we don't unlock as much in men's football – is community, and I think that's the biggest, most powerful thing that we have with football. I love tennis. I love it. I love getting to the gym. I love fitness. But there is nothing that brings people together like football can.

'At elite level, if you sign a new player, it's going to take them a long time to bed in, and why is that? Because you need to build a relationship off the pitch. It's why Manchester United Women took the girls to Malta [at the start of 2023]. It's why Manchester City, every summer and every break, they go away together as a group – because the togetherness of the group is so important to what happens on the pitch. That's why football is so special. So women are finally being able to access this and feel welcomed into this space, and I hate that we still have a huge proportion of society that don't recognise what this can do, how this can improve the world we live in.'

Hardy's own footballing background – as a player and as an administrator – straddled mixed football as well as women's football, meaning she knew what a team dominated by men could be like. It was in marked contrast to the intense concentration she saw with the beginner groups at Manchester Laces, who were all so eager to learn about a sport that was entirely new to them. But Hardy herself had loved playing mixed gender football so much that she had previously stepped away from playing in women's teams, and was driving over to Liverpool every Friday night to play with a mixed team there. She had been considering launching a women-only club, but was not quite sure what she was going to do, or how to brand it, or how to promote it. Her experiences in mixed football helped her to decide.

'I love the boys, but it was like, "I want to do everything that is the opposite of that,"' she recalled, pointing to the kind of casual insults male players would throw at each other, even to their team-mates, either in the guise of pointing out a mistake or under the veil of so-called banter. 'That's the rhetoric that they've grown up with, and on the pitch there's a level of aggression towards each other. You miss a shot, you're mocked. You mess up on a pass – "What the hell are you doing?"

'They treat it differently and I loved it, but I'd played all my life. How can I remove this from whatever I build? Because this, to anybody new coming into the game is just going to kill them, this is going to stop them dead in their tracks.'

She considered how men approached playing mixed-gender matches, suggesting that for them it was just 'another game, but there were some decent footballers that were women playing'. For Hardy and her female team-mate, it was very different.

'I remember saying, "I won't let them push me against the cage today": in women's football that would be a surreal experience. We'd talk about "we've got to pass quicker, because if we don't, he'll be on to us, you've got to be more physical, you've got to lean back in".'

When Hardy went back to playing in all-women teams, she took some of that attitude with her, describing it as a mechanism. The instant she showed some of that behaviour, the other women around her would indicate that it wasn't appropriate.

'It's like, "Well, that's not how we do things around here." It's almost as if – from the elite level down to absolute beginner, just kicked a ball – it's a different game, it's a different sport, a different mentality.'

If a team had a male coach coming across from men's football, she thought, some of that more charged mentality would also make the move, altering the dynamics of an all-female space.

'The language, the rhetoric is winning at all costs. The rhetoric is, "This is what a footballer looks like," "Don't look weak," "Be angry," all these things. You see glimpses of it in the women, you can see the girls acting for the coach, but you can see within that's not why they're there.'

Hardy had seen it in a women's team she tried out before launching Manchester Laces, where the mindset that was encouraged was simply not to be nice. For a new player coming in to an established group, it was not a welcoming atmosphere.

'They didn't want to give me that energy,' she said. '"I'm not here to be nice. We're here to win."'

That was why Manchester Laces took what she described as a 'fresh perspective', with each of the squads, from beginner to competitive 11-a-side, having their own objective under a female-led coaching team. Of course the team competing in the local top division wanted to win the title, but their methods of achieving success and the way they conducted themselves was in contrast to Hardy's former team.

'How are we going to win? By communicating, and being kind to each other, and never bringing in that lad culture,' she said.

One of the other differences she noticed in the women's game was the players' tendency to think less of their abilities than their male equivalents. She likened it to the observation often made about job applications, that women will not send in their CV if they do not have all the qualities and qualifications requested, while men will have a go even if they are lacking some of the requirements. Even Hardy had done this herself in a recent business meeting.

'Somebody said, "You're a footballer as well!" and I said, "No."

'They were like, "Yeah, you are. You play four times a week."

'"No, but I'm not a footballer!"

'"But you play football!"

'"Oh yeah!"

'The reality is I'm a high-level amateur footballer. I play in the top division of Manchester's football scene. I train all the time. I think about it. I love the tactics and all the elements of it. I'm a footballer. Even as a confident woman, which I am, I still go, "No!"'

She saw it also in teams entering themselves in leagues that were aimed at total beginners, and picking up huge wins week in, week out, against squads who were playing matches for the very first time.

'I want to go to these girls and say, "You are so ready to take that next leap, as a team, to challenge yourselves,"' she said. 'I don't think that's a team coming in to try and batter everyone in the league.

'I think it's a team that really hasn't recognised their own strengths as a group, and that they're ready for that next step.'

Hardy was often coaching with the Manchester Laces teams, and took the chance to reflect on her own football journey as well as her practice. She worried that coaches coming into the women's game were not best prepared or best equipped to encourage novice female players to learn the game and enjoy it, and worried that in turn this would mean the huge boom in female participation would drop off very quickly.

'I see it as a real sense of duty, to make them love football and to make them want to stay in football, and I do that by learning their names and learning about their parents and their families, what makes them tick, what makes them uncomfortable. I know which players to pull out for examples, I know which players will be like, "Oh, I'm going to thrive off this," and which players I would never dare to because it will just kill their confidence. I can't fathom that in other amateur teams down the road there are people not learning the players' names at a bare minimum. That's what we're seeing. I'm scared for the women's amateur game because we have a real sense of responsibility now off the back of the Lionesses to empower as many people as possible to want to play.'

* * *

'As one of the more experienced players I did know that there was a lot going on behind the scenes, but until you're actually involved in it, I don't think you realise just how much. When I came in, just looking at things like the organisation that needs to be done, finances that need to be put in place and arranged, it's crazy, the amount of work that does get put in.'

Gemma Sims, once an Oxford United player, had been in post at the club since September as the general manager operating across the girls' section, with all the junior age groups, and the women's first-team set-up. Bringing with her a background in finance – as well as a playing career spent partly in the Women's Super League with Reading – she had hung up her boots as a player with United a few months previously. She had loved her time with the club, but found the time commitment too much to travel from Reading and back for training, especially with a partner who often had work commitments, and with two children of primary-school age who needed childcare in the evenings, and who were also playing football at weekends.

That was not to say she had hung up her boots altogether. She was still playing for Woodley United in the Southern Region Women's Football League, and enjoying a special bonus of her new role – taking up the offer of occasional weekday training sessions with the Oxford United men's first-team coach Karl Robinson. She just wished she had been able to do that while she was still playing for Oxford herself.

'If Karl is running a session at three o'clock, I'll go and join in, just because it's a really good session but it's a fantastic opportunity for our girls to be coached by the first-team manager – they love it!'

Manager Liam Gilbert had mentioned the general manager's job to her, and she sent in her application. Once she had been appointed, she could start to take a more strategic view on how to move the women's team forward.

'He took on a lot, considering he's got a full-time job as a teacher, he did a lot of stuff for the club,' she said. 'I guess it's the same in a lot of clubs in and around our leagues: they have so much potential but they just don't have the people to do it, to put the work in. Liam was trying to get a general manager for a long time because he was trying to do everything by himself; I think he was pretty relieved when they said he could have one, as it does take a lot off his plate so that he can then concentrate more on the team and his sessions.'

As a former player, and a former team-mate of many of the current squad, Sims was in a good position to watch the dynamics of the club, and hoped she could also be a link between all its elements, ensuring good communication and understanding. She was quick to pay tribute not just to Gilbert but the people who kept everything going.

'We've got so many volunteers at the club, who run the matchdays, looking after the gate, refreshments, and they're doing it because they love the game. When you're playing, you know they're there, but you don't really realise exactly what they're giving up for you.'

She had, of course, been impressed with the team's achievements on the pitch so far that season. At the end of January, they were top of the Southern Premier Division, with a two-point advantage plus a game in hand over rivals Portsmouth, in second place. If they held on to that top spot, they would go forward at the end of the season to a play-off against the champions of the Northern Premier Division. The winners of that match would be promoted to the Women's Championship.

'They're doing brilliantly,' she said. 'They came back from Christmas break in really good condition, because they know what's at stake. We've been in this position for a few seasons, and it can turn quite quickly if you're not concentrating on that next game. They're a really good bunch this year. They're working really hard. Liam's keeping them on their toes.'

Improving the club's infrastructure and growing its presence was one of Sims' immediate targets; home attendances had been strong, but now she wanted to increase the number of fans following the team on the road. She wanted more visible marketing in the local area, and possibly in the men's ground, the Kassam Stadium. She was also planning to reach out more to local grassroots clubs and develop stronger links; youngsters were able to walk out with the first team as mascots, but the incredible popularity of that particular opportunity meant that it was booked up months in advance. Sims had already introduced another scheme where children could form a guard of honour for the team and then enjoy a kick-around on the pitch at half-time.

'We're really excited about where we are but there's still a lot of work to be done on the pitch and off the pitch,' Sims concluded.

* * *

'The last time she came to a game she was sick on the way.'

Shelly Provan's daughter Evie suffered badly from car sickness. Added to a three-hour round trip from their house to an Oxford United home game, it was no surprise that the whole family were rarely all there together. Heading to second-tier Bristol City for a clash in the fourth round of the FA Cup was a different matter, and on that occasion Evie walked out on to the pitch hand-in-hand with her mum as one of the team's mascots.

Provan had meant to get both Evie and son Austin Oxford shirts for Christmas, but left it too late, asking manager Gilbert to sort it out in the new year. Evie's new kit arrived just in time for the big cup match, and it coincided with a spell of her being particularly invested in her football as well as a renewed interest in her mum's playing career.

'It was like, "Do you want to come along, be mascot?" and it was a last-minute decision on my husband's behalf because they have rugby in the morning on a Sunday and he drove them all the way down to Bristol for her to be mascot,' Provan explained. Her son had turned down the offer of walking out with the team, preferring to leave the limelight to his sister.

'She came in the changing room, she asked to come back on the team bus, she was in her element, she absolutely loved it,' laughed Provan, who had swiftly been importuned to upload photos and videos of the day on to the school's intranet so all her friends and teachers could see.

Oxford United had enjoyed an incredible streak of form at the start of the 2022/23 season, unbeaten in the FA Women's Premier League Southern Division and putting together cup runs as well. Then they were knocked out of the FA Women's National League Cup by league rivals Portsmouth, 1-0 away a week before Christmas. Despite Evie's support, Bristol City won their Women's FA Cup match 4-0 in the last weekend of January. Then Cheltenham Town handed United their first league defeat of the season the week afterwards, 2-1. It was three defeats out of their last four matches (with a league win over Bridgwater United to start the year), but it was also spread across six weeks, including the festive period. That meant that several players – including Provan, who had missed the Portsmouth match due to a family holiday – had been unavailable for selection. The unbeaten streak had not been uppermost in players' minds, she said, but they were certainly aware they were in good form.

'You definitely do take it one game at a time, but I think you take that confidence into the next game, especially as a back five – we were just saying, "Right, another clean sheet, another win." It was just a mindset: we don't let goals in and we don't lose, not an arrogance, just a confidence in our ability. I don't think we were ever complacent, that was never the case, we always knew that we had to go into every game in the same way and with the same mentality.'

With fixture postponements and cup commitments, Oxford had gained another game in hand over Portsmouth, who were now in the title-winning spot, four points ahead. Sitting on their shoulder suited Provan for the time being.

'Honestly, in everything, in training, whenever we do any practices, I hate being chased, and it's the same for the league,' she said. She had experienced something a little similar with Southampton the previous year, who had also accumulated games in hand, and did not seize the top spot until 10 April, holding on to it until the end of the season and finishing nine points clear of Oxford in second place.

Provan was well aware that Sims and everyone at the men's club were thinking about what might happen next season – what kind of schedule the women's team might have if they got promoted into the second tier, what the squad might look like if they stayed where they were. By the time the 2023/24 season started, Provan would be 39, but was refusing to think that far ahead. She had held off the threat of retirement thus far and was not intending to commit herself to a decision – at least, not yet.

'From a football perspective, at this point I've got to take even every week as it comes, so I don't think I can make any plans for the future,' she said. 'A lot of it is out of my hands in the same way it was last season. I'll play for as long as my body will allow and as long as a manager wants me to play for them.

'For me, I want to be on the pitch for as long as I can. You're retired for a long time, but it's also bringing in family life, work life, so I honestly couldn't tell you. I'm sure Liam would say, "I'm not signing a 39-year-old!"'

She laughed. She clearly knew Gilbert had absolute faith in what she offered the squad, not just as a player but with her experience and her willingness to take on a mentor role with some of the younger players. She demurred, however, when it was suggested that she had played a huge role in ensuring the dynamics in the group were balanced over the season, keeping an eye on the youngsters and keeping everyone on track with their collective focus on promotion.

'In and around the team and the squad, there are [other] people that are more experienced and players that are more experienced,' she pointed out, highlighting her team-mate Naomi Cole, who was about to turn 31 and had played for England at junior age group level. 'Even the ones that are young, their mentality isn't young, they've got their heads screwed on, they're pretty mature for their age.'

Rather than praise individuals, Provan was more interested in what they could achieve as a team.

'[Liam] has put a lot of confidence in me this season, and that's been great,' she said, 'so I've got to focus on that, and on what the job is for this season – to try and get that promotion spot, which is, I think, what the club have deserved for a long time.'

* * *

When Carly Johns scored Oxford United's winner against Billericay Town on 12 February, 14 minutes from time, Gilbert had possibly never cheered so hard in his life.

'Because the games are so stretched out at the minute, it just felt like we lost that thought of how to win, which is a very clichéd thing to say,' he said with a smile. Johns' goal was not just significant on the day, he thought; it was significant in the context of the season and the promotion campaign.

'It relaxed everyone, and just reminded us a bit more of what we're about. We played much better football after that, with a bit more freedom.'

Although Provan was keen to point out the wide age mix in the squad, if not necessarily in the starting line-up, Gilbert was well aware that the inexperience of some of his players meant that they were learning huge amounts from every single game they played, from tactics to how to handle pressure.

'The girls probably overthink it at times as well, because we have got such a young group. We've not been in this position before, so that's why we want to try and take pressure off when we can, but it's understandable when it builds.'

He pointed to his team against Billericay, with the four forward players all aged under 22, and dealing with the opposition's game plan, which was set up to defend in numbers.

'They've never been in these positions before where you're expected to score,' he said. 'The kids – I call them kids – are still getting used to how you process that and learn to deal with that.'

On the plus side, the younger players did not bear the psychological scars of previous campaigns, or bring with them any baggage or disappointment – 'Unless they are those that were here with us last year and we had to watch

Southampton romp the league, [and just] sit there and be a bit helpless,' added Gilbert.

Remembering the extent of the rebuild he had had to do the previous summer, after losing so many of his players, Gilbert found it difficult to remember exactly what his expectations had been from his young squad before the season began.

'We didn't really know how things were going to go. We knew that either we had to go hard on the recruitment if we wanted to go again [for promotion] or we needed to build a younger team to then challenge in a couple of years' time, we seemed to hit this one sweet spot with a bit of both. Obviously players like Shelly and bringing in players like Jenna [Legg, a former Chelsea youth player], Leah [Burridge, who played in the WSL for Yeovil] and those type of players have added brilliant experience to the young core that we've got, so it's just now trying to help them to learn and carry on moving that way – we want to take pressure off of your Shellys and your Nais [Naomi Cole] and people like that so they are not seen as having to lead everything. After the first few games, we thought we've got something special here, and it's just built on from that.'

Although Gilbert had not wanted his players to think about their unbeaten run while they were in the midst of it, it had always been in the back of his own mind.

'Every message that we portrayed to the girls was "on to the next one",' he said. 'Everything was always on to the next one because if we start going at it the other way and then making a big deal of the fact that we were unbeaten, it adds probably a bit of pressure; it just adds something that we don't need, like you don't need to think that way because that's not what got us on that run.

'It's just the next game. We move on to that. Each one is going to be as important as the next one. We've got nine cup finals left; it's that mentality.'

Oxford United were still in a great position to claim that top spot and go forward to the play-off for promotion to the Women's Championship. After winning their match against Billericay, they were still in second place behind Portsmouth, but they were a single point behind, with a game in hand. Gilbert had recently had a meeting with club officials about how his team might operate next season if they did get promoted, and there were several models that could be an option depending on the funding available. Perhaps they would go up after the play-off and switch to a full-time set-up, which would mean Gilbert and many of his players having to decide whether to give up their existing careers to have a shot at genuine professional football, knowing it might only last for a season. Of course, the worst-case scenario was that they would miss out on going up, would lose players, and would have to go through a rebuild again – just as they had done the season before.

'There's a lot of ifs and buts at the moment – we don't really know ourselves,' he admitted. 'I think if we don't go up, yeah, we will probably lose players again. Players will go either to other teams in the league or go and play higher. That's not something to look at just yet, we will know in about four or five weeks' time where realistically if we go on another run of four or five wins, we will know for sure roughly where we will be – but then it's the lottery of a play-off as well.'

Gilbert did not particularly want to think about it, but he knew that promotion was essential if he wanted to keep his best players. Equally, though, he said he would never deny a player the chance to go to a higher level and improve herself if that was an option, even if it did harm his own squad. He reminded his players regularly that ultimately he had their best interests at heart.

'In my opinion, we've got four or five that right now can go and compete in teams in the Championship. There's a few more around that will get there. The same thing happened last year: we lost three players, four players to the Championship. If you don't go up, then you just get pilfered!'

He was joking with his use of the word, but the sentiment was accurate; there was certainly a tremor of foreboding.

'Because the way the game is viewed at our level, you can't hold on to players. You can't say, "I want you for two years" or "we want you for three years" because at the end of May until the beginning of July, they are free agents, no matter what, so anyone and everyone can talk to them.'

He had noticed more players employing agents, despite the fact that the club only paid expenses. It made him more determined to ensure that his players knew that he would always encourage them to move onwards and upwards if they had the opportunity.

'I'm not having you pay money, your hard-earned money, to someone who's going to have their own vested interests. I think that helps, having a bit of transparency with our coaching staff and the players, that they trust that we're doing what we think is best for them.'

Although Gilbert's views were canvassed, the real negotiations about the club's future would be down to general manager Sims, who would liaise with the men's set-up about funding and infrastructure and ultimately the strategy.

'I've seen and talked to managers in the league above, and different models work, different models don't, so I don't know,' he said.

'I don't envy her! Hopefully she can play the politics right and get us moving forward – even more so.'

* * *

Jenna Legg was one of Gilbert's newest recruits, at the start of 2023. She had spent the 2021/22 season with Watford, who had been relegated out of the Women's Championship and into the Southern Premier on the final day of the campaign. The whole season had been somewhat turbulent, coming out of the Covid-induced lockdown and struggling to maintain a rhythm and momentum, resulting in head coach Clinton Lancaster leaving his post in December 2021. After so many months of chaos, it was unsurprising that when the opportunity came for Legg to play in Norway for Amazon Grimstad for three months, she seized it.

'I was like, "This is amazing. I'm going to go live there, three months, finish the season, break out of English football, change of scenery,"' she said.

Though still in her twenties, Legg already had a huge amount of experience. Coming from Basingstoke and playing locally, she joined Chelsea's centre of excellence as a teenager, coincidentally spending time on loan at Oxford in the earliest months of her career. She signed for another WSL side, Brighton & Hove Albion, in 2017, before stepping down to the Championship and Charlton Athletic two years later and then moving on to Watford, with her year there ending in that tough relegation. Though she still loved playing the game, she had become a little disillusioned with football, but friends already at Oxford had told her it was a great place to be.

'I wanted a positive experience. I saw what Oxford were building. I had friends there. They'd all said it was really cool: they're planning to get promoted, they're undefeated, and I was like, "I would love to just go and be a part of that." I think they're a really good club. I spoke to Liam. He was so lovely on the phone and I just thought, "Why not? Why not have a manager who's shown huge interest in me?" He wanted to invest, wanted to improve, wanted to do all these things. "I'm going to go do that, I want to be part of that, hopefully a promotion," all these exciting things.'

Despite her comparative youth, Legg was aware that her experience in the professional game meant that she was going to be one of the role models in the Oxford squad, and that she would need to be helping the younger players through.

'I've heard people say that pressure is a privilege in that way. It's nice to come in with a little bit of [expectation] – it shows that you've had these experiences before and I think that's a good thing. And I'd like to go in and have a positive impact. I want to take all these experiences that I've had in my life – whether that be relegation or playing at a high level – and put them towards something good. It's made me more resilient as a player and I think we're certainly going to need an element of that to get us over the line this season. As much as we've got the results, you need that edge; it comes down to the play-off at the end of the day. That's a huge pressure game. So I think we're going to need a little bit of experience to carry us through it and over the line.'

Having said that, she was not talking about the prospect of promotion with her team-mates quite yet. Just as Gilbert had said, they were treating each game individually as a cup final, and Legg had never been in the situation where she had played for a team that finished top of their league and was not guaranteed promotion.

'I can't imagine winning the league and then you don't go up,' she confessed. 'It's a lot to come down to a play-off. I think that's a huge, huge pressure game for both teams. You have both won your leagues in your own right and then only one of you gets rewarded for it. I think it's really tough.'

Legg was used to tough, though. While a full-time professional at Brighton, she found the long leisure hours did not suit her. Instead, she began a degree in psychology and criminology.

'You're often finished early afternoon and I was like, "What am I going to do?" It sounds ridiculous, and it really is a champagne problem, but I was like, "I don't want to go for coffee every day. It's a really weird lifestyle, and I need something to fill these hours because I can't think about football 24/7." I love studying, I loved doing my A-levels and everything, and I'd always planned to do it so I thought, "Right, now's the time." She was nearing the end of her online degree, and had started training as a test lead for a software company, plus she had also adopted a dog ('Rescue dogs are the best – they're just that little bit extra special'), meaning her life was very busy. Football-wise, though, she had faith in her decision to sign for Oxford United.

'I'd had my experience abroad and I thought that if I'm going to come back, it's got to be for the right environment. I've got to be happy, got to enjoy it. The girls could not have been nicer, they've been so welcoming. It's just an exciting time to be there. Liam's been true to his word. He's been really supportive and for sure it's really lived up to what I hoped. I'm happy.'

9

Knowledge

THE FEBRUARY international window is traditionally the time when teams participate in some form of mini-invitational tournament. In 2022, England hosted their own, known for sponsorship purposes as the Arnold Clark Cup. The three sides making up the inaugural quartet along with the Lionesses were Germany, Canada and Spain – with all four in the top 10 of FIFA's rankings and with the three European sides going into the summer as hopefuls for the European crown. England emerged as the mini-tournament's winners, with one victory and two draws but with four goals scored and a goal difference of +2 giving them the edge over second-placed Spain, highlighting the promise of the team ahead of the summer's Euros. In 2023, they hosted it again, but with slightly less glittering opposition – South Korea, Italy and Belgium, all of whom were, however, still in the top 20 of FIFA's rankings. Once more they won it, with three wins, 12 goals scored, two conceded. This time, of course, nobody needed any additional warning that England would be heading to Australia and New Zealand in the summer with the intention of lifting the World Cup, nor that they had the ability and confidence in the squad to do so.

The achievements of the Lionesses were lauded by their peers and by football industry experts at FIFA's The Best awards on 27 February. Coach Sarina Wiegman was named as the best coach of a women's team and Mary Earps as the best goalkeeper, with Leah Williamson, Keira Walsh, Lucy Bronze and Beth Mead all in the team of the year.

As the Lionesses walked the glamorous red carpet, back at home teams were celebrating lower-profile but no less significant triumphs. Lewes, for example, were enjoying a fruitful run in the FA Cup. In the last weekend of February they beat Cardiff City Ladies 6-1 in the fifth round to reach the quarter-finals, and set up a plum home tie with WSL side Manchester United, one tier higher than them. Assistant manager Natalie Haigh had mixed memories of the FA Cup. As a 17-year-old, she had been part of the Leeds United side that took on the mighty Arsenal in the 2006 final and been thoroughly trounced 5-0 at Millwall's New Den. Although the result did, of course, sting, the achievement of playing in such a big match at such a young age stayed with her.

'I was very shocked to have the opportunity to play,' she recalled. 'That whole season was a little bit of a whirlwind, to be honest, because I'd only played two years of competitive football before that.'

Haigh had 35 family members in the stands cheering her on, including her brother, who flew in from France, where he was then working. She was glad she had some pictorial evidence of the day, because her recollections were hazy – unsurprisingly, bearing in mind the occasion. One somewhat unusual photo had become something of a family heirloom.

'I was never a player that got booked a lot, and I always got told, "As a defender, you should get booked more often,"' she said, 'and I got booked in the FA Cup Final. Arsenal had all these tricky wingers that I was trying to keep up with – I can't remember who it was but I ended up taking her out, and there's a picture that my stepmum took from one stand, where my brother's sitting in the other stand [opposite] and there's not really anyone around him so you can tell it's him and his friend, and the referee is holding up a card to me walking away. That's been framed and left on the family mantelpiece.'

Haigh described Arsenal at that point as unstoppable, but added that as a teenager, playing against such a great side, at a big stadium, for the world's most famous domestic trophy, it was all simply phenomenal. There were, of course, some regrets, apart from the result.

'I'm a bit gutted it wasn't at Wembley,' she confessed. 'There's part of me that wants to get to an FA Cup Final as a coach so I can be at Wembley and experience that.'

Haigh had been pursuing her coaching qualifications while she was still playing, in a career that culminated with Aston Villa in the WSL. She had worked with a local side as an analyst, and coached a junior side, and when she decided to hang her boots up at the end of the 2021/22 season, she was not quite sure what her next steps in football would be.

'I never thought I would know when I was ready to stop playing. I think, to be honest, it just ran its own course. The last couple of seasons were obviously very challenging, both physically and mentally. I only turned pro at the age of 31. The body was struggling a little bit, and psychologically, I went through a promotion and then two pretty intense relegation battles. I realised in myself that maybe I wasn't giving it what it needed and I didn't feel like I could do that anymore. It felt like the right time to step away. It wasn't really planned; I hadn't made the decision at Christmas.

'I just thought, "All I ever wanted was to be a professional footballer, I now don't want to spend the next few years dropping down the divisions." I don't mean that in a rude way, I just felt like I'd taken football as far as I could and was ready to move on.'

Kelly Lindsey, Lewes's head of performance, contacted Haigh to see if she would be interested in the vacant assistant manager position. They had recently recruited former Glasgow City and Birmingham City coach Scott Booth as the women's first-team manager, and were now seeking to get his support staff in post. Haigh was instantly impressed by Lindsey, and liked what she heard about the club.

'I felt like it was a really great project to be a part of,' she said, noting that with a squad consisting mostly of players new to the club along with a new manager and backroom team, it felt like a fresh start and a good time to take on a new challenge. Still, there were additional challenges for her as it would mean time away from her partner and her home in Birmingham. 'It's been difficult being away from home but I guess when you work in football, that's life, isn't it? Sometimes you've got to take opportunities that come.'

This particular opportunity gave her the chance to do plenty of things; the job description for an assistant manager can be different depending on the individual, the manager they work with, and the club they work within. Haigh's duties included game analysis and taking the warm-up on matchdays, plus supporting Booth and taking on any tasks that he perhaps did not have time to do or felt would be better suited to her, along with a few administrative jobs. It also involved an element of pastoral work, which she enjoyed.

'The best part of it is being there for the players. I think I'm quite lucky that I've just come straight off the back of my career, so I can relate to pretty much any problem they're experiencing or things they're thinking. I've played at pretty much every level and haven't played pro for that long, so it's not like I'm going in there as an ex-England international with 500 WSL appearances – I'm pretty real, I'm pretty down to earth and a simple human being that wants to help them in their football journey. That's the best part for me: just working with them and trying to support them to be the best that they can be, really.'

Lewes's emphasis on outreach and attracting new fans to the game meant some unorthodox extra-curricular events. Haigh – and several other coaches as well as players – took part in panel events for novice fans, answering questions they might have about the laws of the game and helping to make them more comfortable in a football environment.

'It's not really something that you'd expect a professional football club to deliver, but the engagement with the people in the room was brilliant. It was so good we did it again.'

Haigh smiled broadly as she explained that women who had been to those evenings were now regulars at the Dripping Pan, and would stop her to ask questions about set pieces and the team's broader tactics.

'Football has always been a massive part of my life,' she said. 'Me and my dad and my brothers used to go watch Leeds when I was a kid growing up. Anything we ever did had football at the heart of it – so many memories. I think it's just a really good sport to bring people together, and that's one thing that Lewes encapsulates really well as a club – that togetherness, that community aspect.'

She recounted a tale from the previous Bonfire Night – always a big occasion in Lewes – and arriving at the ground the next morning four hours before kick-off to find the pitch covered in wooden chips and metal springs from the fireworks that had been set off around the town. She, along with other club staff, began a tough task of clearing the pitch as best they could, conducting a fingertip search, and they were soon joined by 30 to 40 volunteers wanting to help out.

'There were kids, there were men, there were women, there were teenagers, there were staff members. I've never seen anything like it before, but I just had to smile because in the end the game got called off anyway because of rain after Bristol had arrived, which was the most frustrating thing! But the fact that so many people just sort of came to chip in and help out was very Lewes.'

Haigh had been attracted to the club initially by what she understood to be its values, and her months there had only strengthened her feeling that it was the right place for her.

'Everyone that's here has a unique story, which I think we all do, but it's about us coming together and sharing those stories to make us all better and stronger. It's a lovely little town that not many people will have ever heard of. It's a lovely little football club that has the community at the heart of it. That's been my experience of football – most of my best mates I know from football. Everyone's striving for excellence on the pitch but off it as well.

'Maggie [Murphy] and the rest of the staff have so many unique ideas about how the power of football can bring people together and I've always been somebody that really values connections and relationships and closeness and vulnerability and people just authentically being themselves, and I think this is one of very few places I've been that you can – you can do that whether you're a player, a fan, a staff member, a volunteer. The club only operates because of people, and those people are what makes it great. If you come to the Pan or you come to a Lewes event, you'll see that in how it's delivered and how the people interact with anyone that comes – it's just a good bunch of people that want to do good things and want to use the power of football for the better.'

* * *

'We want our crowds to be as diverse as possible and we want as many women as possible to come watch the match.'

Lewes commercial manager Stef McLoughlin was proud of those so-called Offside Rule Nights that the club staged and in which Haigh participated. Attended mostly by women – though not exclusively so – they were able to ask questions which they may not feel comfortable asking a man, or that they did not want to ask in the middle of watching a football match, with the entire event intended to increase their confidence at a football ground.

Club research had also found that female fans were intimidated by some of the traditional aspects of a football ground, such as going in through a turnstile, so they had taken them out and opened the doors wide. McLoughlin made sure she also spoke to people in person to gauge their feelings, and had been saddened by a conversation with a woman who attended every match but still did not feel like a 'real' football fan.

'We had a whole conversation about identity and how hard that can be and how that transitions through time,' she said. 'The women winning the Euros, that was great representation. I was there with my [recreational] football team and we were all in tears at the end of the match because there were women who looked like us, playing football – Alex Greenwood with a face full of make-up – out there being strong. It was just incredible. We love every single minute but it takes time building that into your own personal identity and building it into your own social life. So it's not as easy as just trying to appeal to women.'

McLoughlin started playing football herself after the 2019 Women's World Cup, and found it was a terrific way to make friends. With a grin, she pointed out that she was Lewes's target market – a latecomer to the game, and passionate about the club's values. She had just been editing some documents and crossed out the phrase 'sanitary products', suggesting it should be replaced by the much less prim 'period products' or 'menstrual products'.

'I know I can write that in confidence, because I work somewhere like Lewes,' she said. 'Anywhere else I may not be able to send an email out saying, "I don't want to use the word sanitary." My values link very well to Lewes and the way Lewes does things. I basically get paid to be an angry feminist all day long, which is great.'

The bulk of McLoughlin's job was establishing partnerships with sponsors who wanted to align themselves with the club, ranging from technology companies to fashion brands. Nobody could sponsor just the women's team or just the men's team; all the club's resources were shared. McLoughlin identified possible opportunities and explained to businesses why supporting the club would be beneficial financially and also as a broader part of their brand, potentially as a piece of their corporate social responsibility strategy too. It also meant turning down brands that did not fit with Lewes's own ethos – for example, a gambling firm.

'Anybody who's doing more than just selling a product is who we want to work with, really. We do really, really well with our sponsors because of the sort of club that we are. If you don't have a strong ethos, I don't think you're going to want to support Lewes; you support Lewes because you want to shout out about how strong your company values are.'

Of course, following the Lionesses' win, there had been some increased interest in sponsoring a club with such a clear stance on equality, and where the women's team was competing at a higher level than the men's. There had also been some new difficulties raised by the slick public relations exercises that had been continuing at the highest level, with so much mainstream media attention on the England players, by now regulars on red carpets – with Chloe Kelly recently presenting an award at the Brits.

'There's one thing that is slightly problematic,' McLoughlin pointed out. 'If you don't know football, if you don't know women's football – I hate calling it women's football but I'm having to – if you're just an average Joe, just watched bits of the Euros, saw the publicity, saw Jill Scott on television, like loads of people I'm pitching to, [you'd] say, "Oh, but women's football is fine! Everything's OK, you won the Euros, it's all OK. The world is fine. We have equality now." That is the perception of a lot of brands we speak to.'

Explaining the reality of women's football – even in the second tier of elite competition, where Lewes were comfortably situated – was something McLoughlin needed to do regularly. Although Lewes's women were treated the same as their men and vice versa, the same could not be said of many other clubs.

'People are shocked when they find out women don't play on the same pitches as men. They don't understand. When you talk about the actual inequality that we face at the moment, people are still quite shocked when they realise that women still don't make much money even at a really high level, they are one injury away from their careers ending. People are still really shocked by that. So you have to double-explain it and just explain it and explain and explain to them.'

Lewes's targets for sponsorship and for attendances were already ambitious prior to the Lionesses' success, so that single event did not change their aims. They concentrated on making the Dripping Pan a place that felt welcoming for a non-traditional football audience – offering drinks other than beer, for example, and food other than a pie or a burger. All these plans and projects cost money, and it meant that McLoughlin's work was never done.

'We are very ambitious,' she agreed. 'Because of the whole concept of "women's football is doing great", and also Lewes are in the media a lot, a lot of people think we're doing really great, but we do still need a lot of support. Operational costs are really high in everything we stand for. We spend a lot of time working on our impact outside of the football club as well. So all of that's obviously really expensive, so we'd love to be supported by a couple more bigger brands.'

She was darkly amused by some of the comments she still got from people surprised that she worked in football, but at the same time it reminded her why she did her job.

'I've had three people ask – three men ask – whether I like football. I play football. I work in football. If I was a man you wouldn't be asking me whether I like football. If I was a man, they'd probably be like, "Oh my God, that's so cool. You get to work in football!"'

* * *

Kate Chesser's work with London Seaward was, she thought, the perfect job. She had just been appointed as their mental coach using the sport psychology degree she had earned three decades earlier along with qualifications in other complementary techniques. She had been working with elite athletes as well as amateur, but wanted to contribute her skills to the sport she loved.

'Tennis was my main sport, but I grew up with football – watching it, because at my age, it really was not ...' She paused. 'My mum and dad would not have encouraged it. Fine in the backyard with my brothers, but really, I didn't know it was a thing, it wasn't something girls could do that I knew of, anyway – of course they could.

'Then I was a tennis player but got diagnosed with MS [multiple sclerosis] and didn't play for about 15 years. I play wheelchair tennis now; the psychology of it was massive, going from winning and being good, not amazing, but a good club player, to really crap and then having to deal with that.'

That was the trigger to revisit and add to her mental coaching skills, and she realised that she would be able to make a big difference to a women's football club.

'When I go to turn on the TV, what do I look for first of all? Football, even more so than tennis, to be honest. I was scrolling through Twitter and saw [London Seaward's] post about ACL injuries, and how if this was a man at a similar level in men's football, they would be whisked off the pitch, have it scanned, and off for repair, whereas the women have to wait for months and months. I went to their website to have a look. It's got inclusion splattered all over it and being a wheelchair user myself – I held a place on the LTA [Lawn Tennis Association committee] Middlesex for inclusion, trying to make sports inclusive – I just thought, "Oh my God, this club's fantastic."'

Chesser got in touch with the club offering her services, and when she spoke to manager Dan McKimm she got on with him instantly. Within days she was part of the backroom team, attending every home game and as many away ones as were feasible.

McKimm's vision for the club was enticing to Chesser, who did not need too much persuasion to join. One of the initiatives she was working on was an injury clinic offering support for players who were out for an extended period of time, such as those with anterior cruciate ligament injuries – the struggles of whom had caught her attention when she first learnt of Seaward and their work.

'It's the questions, the doubt, the waiting for the operation, not knowing what's going to happen.'

Chesser listed off the difficulties that footballers on the sidelines had to cope with, adding, 'And yeah, coming to the games. It takes a while to be able to come to the games because of the emotional trauma of the injuries and the not knowing. It is massive to have that together.'

She drew on her own experiences to support those women. 'It's obviously not an ACL injury, but when I was diagnosed with MS, not being able to play tennis, you think all the things – it's just not fair. It's heartbreaking, basically. Why should you go through it alone?'

She offered one-to-one consultations with players who requested it as well as a group session for the squad on topics such as goal-setting, self-belief and confidence.

'It's just another muscle you have to train,' said Chesser of the brain, adding that it was a bit of a challenge to get the entire squad to buy in to some of the exercises, particularly the ones that leant more towards the complementary medicine side of things, but as they began to see the results it was much easier to get buy-in. She admitted to feeling a sense of impostor syndrome – that she did not deserve to be working alongside these athletes – but that the players and staff had been very welcoming.

'It has been amazing. I can do this full-time. I feel like I've missed my calling – or found my calling. Yeah, I'm not past it yet! These ladies – they're all high achievers, not just the football but off the pitch as well. They've all got so much good stuff going on, they're fitting training and matches in around school, college, jobs, family commitments, all the things. Your mental health is such a big part of [success]; they really do need support. They are a good team, they have got each other, but just having that extra piece of support and being able to help that is fantastic.'

It had also made Chesser think about her own mental health and how she dealt with challenges, an opportunity she had not expected when she took up the role.

'I need to work on my own mental game as well: stop feeling awkward, get rid of that impostor syndrome, because actually the feedback I'm getting has been great. The ladies that have been slightly sceptical [about the value of mental coaching], they're very nice about it, and they're open about it – not in a horrible way, just a questioning way, which is good. It makes me ultimately accountable.'

The results suggested that Chesser's contributions were making a difference to Seaward's form on the pitch. Since the start of 2023, Seaward had lost a Capital Women's Cup match on penalties, but in the league they had strung together enough good results to inch their way into the top four.

'They're reaping the rewards, the benefits coming through,' she said. 'It's the best employer, and then the other best thing about is when you see the results on the pitch. I love it, because I'm quite results-driven but footballers also are because they want to win. I know it's all about playing well and all the other stuff too, but we want to win, or, at least do our best to win anyway. It's very rewarding.'

10

Confidence

MADDIE JONES had scored 22 goals in 13 games for Shrewsbury Town in the 2022/23 season. It was her firepower that had helped them to the title in Division One North of the West Midlands Women's Regional League the year before – with 35 goals in 22 appearances. How would Jones describe her current run of form?

'Not too bad,' she demurred. 'Last season was a really good season, not just for myself, but for the team as well because we got promoted, an unbeaten season, so you can't really complain, but I didn't expect really to go into this season scoring as many goals as I did [last year]. Not looking too bad so far. So ...'

She paused, and smiled a little. Shrewsbury's form had been a little inconsistent, with a draw against bottom-of-the-table Coundon Court Ladies at the end of January, followed by a home defeat to league leaders Kidderminster Harriers. Since then, though, they had started to string together some wins to close in at the top of the table. With just one promotion spot available, it could be too much to ask, but Jones was determined they would be giving it their best shot, wondering if it could go down right to the end of the season.

'Teams around us are drawing to teams that you wouldn't expect them to; I mean, we drew with the bottom of the league, which we were a bit gutted with, but you're still seeing it with the other teams around us. They are losing points against teams [where] you didn't really expect them to be losing points. They could fall to anyone!'

Jones was a Shrewsbury girl. She had begun playing as a very small child, attending a camp run by the club's community foundation during the school holidays, and her only memory of the day was sobbing because she was the only girl there, and she did not want to join in a session with a group of boys, despite her father's desperate attempts to encourage her. It did not traumatise her for too long; she joined a local team, and then became part of Shrewsbury Town's Centre of Excellence. However, her time there was truncated; due to funding issues, her team folded. Several of the parents of the girls who had been at the centre of excellence created a new team for them, and Jones signed up. She could have looked for another centre of excellence, she thought, with a clear pathway to the top of the game, but at that point she had lost her confidence.

'At that age, you just want to really play, don't you? You'll do anything you can to play and that's what I did. I wasn't enjoying it too much when I came away from the centre of excellence, so I didn't go into that academy route because my mum and dad, at that age, they wanted to get my confidence back up before taking me into that or trying to get me back into that environment because you'd just be

174

getting knocked down, I think, if you went in there with no confidence. So they formed our own team, like a local team [where I] could carry on playing with my friends and that's what I wanted to do at the time.'

Jones had found it difficult to find her place in a high-performance academy, and struggled with the variable expectations between coaches – some wanting every player to have equal game time, and some wanting to pick the best players every single time. Not knowing quite where she stood as a footballer had affected her, but she also thought that her personality meant she was prone to losing confidence and taking criticism to heart. She accepted that others might be shocked by that when they saw her scoring so many goals, but pointed out that she was scoring goals because she was happy and enjoying herself.

'I take things quite personal[ly], and that's not just in football, that's across life,' she said. 'Ella Toone or Leah Williamson, if someone says something to them, they'll shrug it off. I don't know if it's just because we're all so friendly [in the league] or obviously we're all local – I don't know if that's the reason [I] take it a bit more personal. I don't mean to, but that's something that I do. It could be people on the team, it could be the coaches, and I know they're trying to help but sometimes I just feel like, "I know where I've gone wrong. I don't need somebody else to tell me," especially at this age now, I'm a bit more experienced within football. I know they're trying to do their job but it's a bit hard, isn't it?'

Jones was 23. After spending a couple of seasons with her former centre of excellence team-mates in Church

Stretton, she was scouted for Welsh side TNS, who signed her up for their junior section and promoted her to the senior team as soon as she turned 16. After that, she played for AFC Telford, but it was always her home-town club who held her heart.

'Growing up in Shrewsbury, being a Shrewsbury fan, I wanted to play for Shrewsbury,' she said. When the women's side started up again and was taken in under the club's community arm, she knew she would head back there. She was a qualified PE teacher, working in a local school, and combining that with playing football for Shrewsbury was the culmination of her childhood dream.

'Women's football now has got much bigger – in the top leagues you can have it as a full-time job. But when I was younger, it was always, "I'm going to be a professional footballer, but obviously I can't be full-time so I'll be a PE teacher as well." That's always been actually what I wanted to do, football and PE, and it's worked out.'

For someone who took even constructive criticism personally from a very young age, going into teaching had meant she took her own experiences to the job and gave herself a fresh perspective on how to work with young people, and encourage girls in particular into the sport she loved so much.

'You've got to bear that in mind when you're teaching, and to try and give everybody a bit of the same sort of level, and try and push everybody because people are all at different abilities. That's the same with football, especially grassroots football. You've got people that are just wanting to start up, you've got people that have been playing since they were younger. At the minute we're trying to promote girls' football a lot more at the school that I'm at, and it's great when you've got young girls coming up to you and saying, "Oh, I've just joined a football team," or, "I want to come to football!" and it's really nice. Then on the other hand, you don't want them to come into it and then have girls that might have been there a bit longer and just being like, "You're rubbish," or "You're not as experienced, we don't want you in the team." So you've got [to create] that level playing field, making sure that everyone's respectful to each other because they all want to be in the same environment.'

Jones's goalscoring exploits were well known at school, and her pupils were keen to cheer her on in person if they could. Even if they were not at a game, though, Shrewsbury's strong social media presence meant the young people could keep up to date with what had happened.

'We're not professional, but it's nice to still get that recognition. You've got kids, not even the girls but the boys as well, walking past me in the corridor at school and to be like, "Seen you on TikTok, Miss, seen you score this goal," and it's just great.

'I know a lot of female footballers, especially in our level, are PE teachers, just because that's what they want to do. It's great that in school, kids have got that role model as a PE teacher, that actually plays sport.'

Jones was settled and happy, loving her football and playing at a good level for the club she had always wanted to represent. Of course, her goalscoring record had drawn plenty of attention from other clubs – not just in Shrewsbury's league, but at a higher level. Nevertheless, she was intending to stay with the Shrews for the foreseeable future. She got on well with her team-mates and they had a great understanding on the pitch, and the training requirements fitted in well around her commute to and from work in Telford. Other clubs in higher leagues would be training three or four evenings a week plus a match on a Sunday and it simply would not be possible for her even if she wanted to do it.

'It's just like, "I'm busy being a teacher!" – and obviously you have to have that extra commitment as well, fixtures after school. So if I'm working until half four, and then we've got to be at training for half six, and it takes me an hour to get there, it's just chaos!

'Shrewsbury have progressed so much over the last couple of seasons. You're lucky to get a set-up like that at our level.'

Wolverhampton Wanderers, for example, were about an hour's drive away. They were in the third tier, and had handed out that sound FA Cup beating to Shrewsbury earlier in the season. Jones thought the match had been instructive not just for the team's immediate progress, but to consider how the club could develop in the future; although the club had begun to look at its pathway for younger girls, there was still not a direct replacement for the centre of excellence that Jones had played for as a child.

'It was a great opportunity to play against Wolves, just to show where we want to be at in the future and what we need to do in order to get to that place, whether that's how we play on the pitch or maybe having a development squad, or the academy, the centre of excellence.

'That's where we differ from Wolves, because they've got that academy, they've got that set-up to then literally come from a young child all the way up into the women's team, and even if you're not getting into the women's [first team], you've got the reserves or your development squad.'

Shrewsbury had under-16s, but Jones wondered whether there needed to be an older age group as well, to help young players progress from junior football to the first team. She also acknowledged that in a relatively small town, it might be a difficult thing to introduce, whereas Wolves, Birmingham City and Aston Villa benefited from each other's proximity.

'If [players are] not getting into one of the academies then they will go try for the other academy and they're not that far away from each other, whereas Shrewsbury, we haven't got that sort of set-up to be able to link with other academies. If people maybe don't get into the West Brom one, they're going to go to the likes of Wolves or Aston Villa. They're not going to say, "I'll go to Shrewsbury," because we haven't got that set-up.'

It was something Jones knew the club wanted to do, but there were anxieties about the number of players it would attract. She, however, was adamant that it would be a success for the girls who, like her, just wanted to represent their home-town club with pride.

* * *

'It's something we're chatting about at the moment, with the direction of the team,' confirmed manager Tom Peevor. 'We are foundation-run and two years ago that really helped us because they took away the fees [for players to pay] and gave us a great pitch and stuff like that. The problem you've got is you have to remember it's a charity, so they have to be really careful.'

He gave the example of player payments; Shrewsbury Town did not pay their players, but he thought that if they were going to compete at a decent level, they were going to have to consider it. He had tried to attract loan players locally but had problems convincing players to make the journey to Shrewsbury when no money was on offer.

'We've actually got a good reputation,' he added. 'I was chatting to someone from West Brom the other night, and they were like, "We know if we send our players to you they are going to be looked after, everything is correct in terms of coaching and environment, but you're just a bit out of the way and there's no money involved." So that's a big threat to us. I think going forward, especially if we do get promoted, we're going to have to have some kind of financial backing to keep on pushing.'

By the second week of March, Shrewsbury were third in the table – five points behind new leaders Sutton Coldfield Town, and one point behind Kidderminster Harriers, who had drawn twice in the league in February and dropped out of the sole promotion slot.

'You have to lose a maximum of one game to get up, really,' said Peevor, whose side had already lost two. 'You've got to win the rest.

'It's pretty tight at the top. The vibe I was getting from the team was, "We're not going to win the league now, we've lost it," but since we've had a bit of a winning streak and bounced back, I feel like they're, "Ooh, we've got a chance now." So all we can do, like I said to the team, is concentrate on ourselves. As long as we are getting three points each week, we put pressure on other teams.'

Peevor had always expected his team to do well in the Premier League after their runaway success the previous year. What came as a surprise was not coming up against better teams, but against weaker teams, with worse and smaller pitches: 'Sometimes those games are uglier,' he explained.

'A lot of our tiers, one goes up, one goes down. That's why you have so many teams that stay in the league for so long, just because [only] one goes down. In our league, for example, there are a couple of teams that I think are actually really well run, organised, hard to beat, and then there's quite a few that are still in that old "put together a team and hope for the best" style.'

The resurgent belief in the team – exemplified by Jones's evident confidence – gave Peevor plenty to be happy about. His entire tenure with the club had been a learning curve, he knew, and a challenging but successful season after a dominant promotion campaign had given him and his players more to think about.

'I've seen the group evolve, and I've evolved with them really,' he said. 'That's what I've really enjoyed: more than getting promoted, more than the wins, it's been me getting stuff wrong, learning from it, but also the players as well.

'We're in it together, and I feel like they're happy to be there. They probably aren't completely honest with me, because they want to be picked, and I get that, but I feel like they are pretty honest with me, and will say things to me that maybe need changing but it's for the good of the team, it's not just to be horrible, and I feel like there's a real nice balance of that within the squad really – they feel confident enough to do that. That's really helped me personally, because there [have] been things I've got wrong this season; trying to manage a team who have just come up and who are used to winning so much does present challenges in itself. But they're open enough to feed that back to me and in a good way and improve the team, and that's been a massive help for me and helped me to enjoy the journey.'

* * *

International Women's Day 2023 was, inevitably, a day chosen for plenty of announcements as companies pledged to promote sex equality in opportunity and in practice. Wednesday, 8 March also went down in the history books as the day that the Lionesses won another great victory, perhaps one even more glorious, striking and long-lasting than the trophy they had lifted at Wembley the previous summer. The government and the FA announced the success of the squad's campaign that had begun with an open letter to the prime ministerial candidates in the autumn, with a commitment to provide girls in England with equal access to football in schools. The government made the declaration as part of what they termed an 'all-sports' pledge – telling schools they should deliver a minimum of two hours of PE every week and ensure that girls had the same opportunity to play every sport as boys, including football. They also announced an increased investment in school sport and after-school activities, detailing more than £600 million over two years for the PE and Sport Premium and £22 million for the School Games Organisers network, intended to allow schools the ability to plan ahead and ensure an inclusive curriculum of sport.

Of course, the governing body's executives were prominent in the announcement, with Mark Bullingham, the FA's chief executive, quoted in the press release as saying: 'The magic of last summer's Euros victory can now live on with a legacy that has the ability to change the future of women's football and positively impact society. Equal access for girls is one of the FA's strategic ambitions and for such progress to be made is a very proud day.'

Baroness Sue Campbell, the FA's director of women's football, was quoted as saying: 'As soon as the final whistle was blown at Wembley on 31 July 2022, the players turned their attention to what they wanted their legacy from the tournament to be and what's been announced today is as important as anything that was achieved on the pitch in the summer.'

She added: 'A conversation led by Lotte Wubben-Moy and Leah Williamson on the bus from the Trafalgar Square celebrations has today delivered real change in society and the announcement is testament to their tenacity and excellent engagement with the government. The FA are as proud of them as we have ever been.'

Williamson's quote demurred, handing the credit to Wubben-Moy.

'The success of the summer has inspired so many young girls to pursue their passion for football. We see it as our responsibility to open the doors for them to do so and this announcement makes that possible. This is the legacy that we want to live much longer than us as a team. On behalf of all the Lionesses players, we'd like to thank our team-mate Lotte Wubben-Moy as a driving force behind this transformational change. We couldn't be prouder to stand alongside her and we all look forward to seeing the impact this legacy creates.'

Wubben-Moy's quote was characteristically straight to the point.

'By making football more accessible to millions of girls across the nation, we have opened a crucial door for the growth of women's football and women's sport as a whole. I am proud to be part of something that will live on for generations to come. This is just the beginning.'

She expanded in an open letter published on the Arsenal website that she learnt about the way the world ran during those football matches, but she also learnt about herself, with her confidence and motivation increasing, and realising in retrospect that plenty of the girls who walked past them and did not want to join in may simply have lacked the confidence to do so. However, that was not the only thing that dissuaded potential footballers.

'As I grew up the street was traded for real pitches. The football teams I was part of moved predominantly outside of the M25. This meant that the once-post-school run around the corner was replaced by an ever-growing dependence on my privilege; my mum would drive me to training three or four times a week, often taking along other girls from the local area with us. We could afford the many and frequent team payments, new boots, and match fees. And most importantly I always had my parents' full support.

'But I know there will be so many girls out there who are not so lucky. Having witnessed it first hand, I know this necessity to travel has already ended so many young players' careers in London and perhaps stopped many more from ever beginning.'

She added: 'Imagine how many future Lionesses you could pick out in every playground across the nation with every school now offering equal access to football.

'Well, that is now the reality the Lionesses squad of 2022 dreamt of. But the victory is so much greater than that, because many don't play football dreaming of a professional career. It's the camaraderie, the adrenaline, and the endorphins that I felt as a young girl. It is the teamwork, the social networking, and the lifelong friends made on the pitch. It is the beautiful game that I know so well.'

11

Equality

LEWES, ALWAYS the flag-wavers for equality and never afraid to take a stance, had campaigned for years on the topic of FA Cup prize money. Indeed, they had launched their Equal FA Cup campaign in 2019, describing the disparity between the men's and women's prize money as 'a gaping eyesore amongst the world's major sporting competitions'. The Lewes board of directors had written an open letter to their FA counterparts in February 2019, praising their 'For All' strategy, and highlighting the opportunity to use the cup as 'an ideal mechanism for financially irrigating the women's game', just as the men's cup was always used as a way of redistributing wealth to the grassroots.

They issued an impressive clarion call: 'Let's get these prize funds to a level that we would all be able to tell our children about without embarrassment ... That would at a stroke increase the level of focus and seriousness paid to the women's game by existing clubs by an order of magnitude.'

As many observers had pointed out in 2022 upon the announcement of an increased prize fund for the women's cup, the men's prize fund had expanded at the same time, but at a higher rate, meaning the gap between the two had actually increased. When Lewes got a plum home draw in the FA Cup quarter-final – at home to giants Manchester United – Lauren Heria's mind started racing. She went into the club the next day to speak to CEO Maggie Murphy, who assured her that if she wanted to do something under the Equal FA Cup banner, she would get all the support she wanted.

'She spoke to me about what they'd done before, and straight away my mind was like, "I feel there would be so much power if we'd do something that was player-led,"' she said. 'She was like, "If you want to do it, do it!"' Heria spoke to club captain Rhian Cleverly and some of the senior players in the squad, and pitched her idea of a player-led open letter. With their support, she put together a presentation about the inequality of the FA Cup prize money that she gave to the players and staff.

'By the end of the presentation, we were like, "Does anyone have any questions?" We didn't get any questions back, but what we did get was a lot of support, and all the players in the room were like, "We want to do this, what do we do next?"' Twenty-three-year-old Willa Bailey had been elected on to the board back in October; Lewes's commitment to doing things differently, in an equitable way, extended to encouraging young people to take up directorships and to ensure that any required meetings were organised in the evenings rather than during the work day, which would be less accessible to someone less well established in their career. She had been thrilled to see

Heria and the rest of the players express their desire to take the lead on this latest iteration of the Equal FA Cup campaign.

'The players did it themselves,' she said. 'They came up with the idea, and it wasn't like a higher power saying, "We think you should do this, it'll look good. You should maybe have this conversation." It's ingrained in them.'

Indeed, Heria never had any doubt that the squad would pull together. She praised the leadership skills of Cleverly in particular, and although her time at Lewes was her first spell in a professional club, she thought that the dynamic in the club contrasted with some of the semi-professional set-ups she had been part of.

'I feel the difference here. It really feels like everyone wants to support each other and bring the best out of the players. "This is important – can you listen?" People listen.'

With captain Cleverly, centre-half Nat Johnson and goalkeeper Laura Hartley, Heria drafted the open letter addressed to former England international Karen Carney, appointed by the government to lead a review into the future of women's football.

'We are proud to drive the game forward, but we ask for fair reward,' they wrote. '#EqualFACup sends a clear signal to society: female footballers deserve equal recognition and reward. Sharing the total combined prize fund equally between men and women has the power to be transformative in the women's game. It would allow clubs to invest more funds in player wages, facilities, equipment, medical care, staffing, travel costs, and everything the women's football pyramid needs to thrive and grow. Put simply, it will allow

us to focus on football.' They signed off: 'Keep the magic –
just make it equal.'

They did not get a swift response from Carney or those
in positions of authority, but they certainly caught the
attention of football fans and the media. With the help of a
national newspaper, and the backing, of course, of Lewes's
men's team, they achieved plenty of coverage, and gained
hundreds of signatures supporting their call for an equal
prize pot. Lewes lost their quarter-final 3-1, but took a great
deal of pride in what they had achieved during that cup run
both on the pitch and off.

'The players really felt like they got to use their voice,
and the club helped them to do that,' said Heria. 'It was
really nice that we pulled together as players, men and
women. The men's team are super with it, our board's been
very supportive. Although obviously we haven't got what
we wanted in terms of a response, in terms of any sort of
commitment around equalling the prize pot, the thing it did
allow us to do is really come together as one club in order
to show the world what women's football can be and what
Lewes is. I think that was a really fun and exciting thing
to be a part of.'

Heria could not help but compare the experience to what
she and her Leyton Orient team-mates had gone through
when they tried to raise awareness of their situation as they
separated from the men's club of the same name.

'We made a lot of noise there [at Orient, but] I definitely
had more sleepless nights last year. I stand by both those
campaigns, I stand by them both equally. I think the
difference was when it was Leyton Orient I felt very much

on my own – I felt our players were on our own, we didn't have the support we needed, whereas with Lewes, I never felt like I was on my own. I always felt like there was someone fighting my corner and, yes, it was my team-mates. I definitely had that at Leyton Orient, but I think it was an extra layer from the club and people who have more of that professional background in that space.'

Heria's contribution and dedication was recognised by everyone within the club. She picked up their weekly internal award, 'Lewes Legends', for three weeks on the bounce as she worked on the project. It gave her some consolation; she had not been playing regularly for the first team, and she was out of match practice. She had known when she signed for the club that she would not be able to command a place in the starting eleven immediately, but had hoped to be able to work her way in. However, in the competitive second tier of women's football in England, manager Scott Booth had continued to seek to strengthen his squad, adding players during the transfer window who had a lot of experience at a higher level than Heria. It was ironic that it was during the Equal FA Cup campaign that she began to realise and accept that she would perhaps not be able to get the footballing experience that she wanted at Lewes at the present time. Following a chat with assistant manager Natalie Haigh ('she's very good at listening to us as players, validating us, helping us figure out an action path'), she spoke to Booth, and they discussed the idea of a dual registration, enabling Heria to go and play for a team who would normally have a match on the same day as Lewes.

'He said to me, "You've really improved a lot this season,"' she recalled. 'He was really good about it, we had a good chat. I feel like he has invested in me as a player. He was like, "I'm happy to see you go out with your agent and have conversations with as many clubs as you want and come back to me when you have got an idea, and I would like to be involved in terms of making sure that it's a club that I feel will develop you."'

Heria signed on a dual registration for AFC Wimbledon in the FA Women's National League Division One South-East. In another layer of irony, her first match with her new club was a top-of-the-table clash against London Seaward, who had grown from the ashes of Leyton Orient Women, the team she had fought to keep alive in its previous incarnation. It ended in a 1-1 draw, with Seaward equalising in the closing seconds. Heria came on as a second-half substitute for the last 22 minutes.

'I still have a very good relationship with all the girls and staff there, they were really supportive,' she said. Since then, she had been named in the starting line-up for Wimbledon's next two matches; they had won both to close the gap on Hashtag United, in the automatic promotion spot, and pull away from Seaward, sitting in third. 'It's been amazing to see how much I've developed as a player, so it's nice. I got player of the match last game [a 2-1 victory over Cambridge City], which was cool. It's been really good getting the minutes and being able to contribute on the pitch. It's a good group.'

She acknowledged that the last season, difficult though it may have been, had contributed hugely to her development as a player. 'As much as it's not necessarily worked out how I wanted on the pitch at Lewes, it's definitely a club I speak very highly of. I like how the Championship is developing.'

Heria was already looking ahead. She was thinking about playing in continental Europe in the future, and felt that her progress over the last season would equip her well for that. She also thought that the challenges she had faced, coping with and learning about a professional football environment and campaigning on issues that were important to her, had helped her to develop as a person.

'I definitely feel it's probably the most stressful environment I've been in, for sure!' she laughed. 'I think that's taught me a lot about me, particularly in the earlier days, when in my head I felt like I was really off the mark in terms of football, nowhere near where I needed to be, for myself and for the team. I always put a lot of pressure on myself but there was definitely times when I thought, "Maybe I should just quit, it would be easier." Obviously I didn't.

'I'm happy with how I've developed, I'm happy that I feel I've had a positive impact on players and the squad and the club as a whole. In many ways it's been a really huge success, something I'm glad I've done.'

* * *

One of the players benefiting from Seaward's developing professional approach was Zahmena Malik, who had made her senior international debut for Pakistan, assisting a goal as she played all 90 minutes against Comoros. International honours were naturally relatively rare for players in the fourth tier; she had been spotted in a pre-season friendly by a coach who had links with the national set-up and referred her to the management, and she was thrilled to be able to represent the country. With international duty, her training and games with Seaward, plus a coaching career, her life revolved around football.

Malik – known as 'Zee' to her friends and team-mates – had begun playing properly as a small child, but even as a toddler she had loved running around in the garden kicking a ball around, even if it was just by herself. She had signed for Seaward around a year previously, and even in that short time she could see the club's progress.

'We've improved drastically, and that's hats off to the amazing coaching staff, who put a lot of effort, time and care into taking the club to where it is right now, and alongside the coaching staff, we have players who really care about the club and the direction of where they would like to take [it],' she said. 'It's been great to witness and be a part of a club who not only want to get better at football but care about being great individuals off the pitch.'

London Seaward, as an independent club, were always preparing contingency plans, just in case option A fell through or they found themselves gazumped by someone with deeper pockets. They were looking ahead to next season expecting to be in a new home by the time they began their fixtures. As Heria had discovered, they were a formidable side to face, playing out that thrilling draw against second-placed AFC Wimbledon at the end of March, but despite their exploits on the pitch, they were not secure in their Walthamstow home, Wadham Lodge.

The ground's primary tenants Walthamstow FC posted on Twitter at the start of February, entitled 'Walthamstow FC Women need you!' The post called for 'a women's team to join [them] on [their] journey', and sought expressions of interest 'if you are an existing women's team who would like to represent E17'. Seaward, who had shared their ground for two years, were not mentioned. They were, of course, committed to keeping their own name and remaining separate from any men's club; part of their entire ethos was to operate as a sustainable, standalone club only for women, not reliant on any philanthropy from a men's team.

'Having been in that kind of marriage before as a club [as Leyton Orient] and seen how it ends, we have no desire to be in that kind of situation again,' explained vice-chair Gareth Edwards – a Leyton Orient season-ticket holder himself. 'The women's game shouldn't just be the same teams that you see in the men's game. That's not progress. That's just cloning. We lose the identity of the women's game if it's exactly the same.'

A women's team, wherever it is a tenant, will invariably find itself getting the second choice of everything, from pitch availability to training facilities. Edwards was well aware of this problem; if Seaward did not have a permanent home with some degree of autonomy, their ability to plan for the long term would be restricted.

'This is the problem we face as a club trying to establish ourselves, and that's not unique to women's football.' He gave the example of the club formerly known as Wimbledon, who in the 1990s had to leave their home at Plough Lane due to the expense that making it adhere to new safety standards would incur, and had to ground-share with nearby Crystal Palace at Selhurst Park. 'If you don't have your own place, a place you can call your own, you can't build a community and you can't build a fan base and you can't expect players to want to play for you and everything else. So our goal is and always has been to find somewhere where we can know we've got the stability of calling home, and that is a common problem for all women's clubs in London because we don't get pitch priority and the pitches aren't there. London [City] Lionesses play in Dartford; they're the largest [independent] London women's team, yet they can't play in London. If we as a game can't start getting homes for women's clubs – permanent homes or at least long-term lease homes – we have no future.'

Lots of women's teams in east London had cast covetous eyes over the abandoned Hare and Hounds ground, the former home of the since-dissolved Leyton FC. Plenty of proposals had been put together to create a mecca for the women's game in the area, with a decent amount of political will behind it from the local authorities, but as always funding was an issue. Edwards was hopeful that at some point in the future the project may begin moving forward, and just had to keep fingers crossed that a team like Seaward would be considered as a potential priority tenant.

'You anchor that out on a club like us,' he suggested, 'and then what you don't do is let Tottenham Women into it, you don't let Leyton Orient Women into it, because all you're doing with them is you're boosting brands that can already boost themselves.'

London Seaward's intentions for the next season were to move a few tube stations down the line to Barkingside, and ground-share with Redbridge FC. They were discussing a ten-year lease, which would give Seaward security as well as priority over the pitch on a Sunday, meaning they could decide their own kick-off times. Redbridge were also working towards the installation of a next-gen (artificial) pitch, which, when ready, would mean that Seaward could potentially arrange an entire day of women's football, with the reserves playing on one pitch in the morning, and the first team playing in the main stadium in the afternoon.

'You can get people down there, you can say, "Well, come and watch us, come build a thing. We're going to be there every Sunday. You're not going to have to sit there watching our Twitter account working out whether we've been rained off for the third week in a row." It's about giving us an opportunity to start building a fan base and a community around the club.'

He hoped that Barkingside would welcome Seaward, and he had a personal ambition to have the tube station give the club a dedicated roundel – one of the London Underground's iconic symbol signs, stating the name of the station along with something like 'Home of London Seaward FC'.

'It pains me every time I go to work, and I go via Leyton [tube] station, and every single bit across those [ticket] barriers, every single bit down that platform isn't even Leyton Orient Women, it is Spurs Women [who shared the Orient men's Brisbane Road ground], because the Super League has proportionately got the money. They blanket the advertising. If you can't win the advertising war in your own borough, what hope have you got as a club?'

Of course, Seaward were sad to be leaving Walthamstow. They were very grateful for their time there; when they had begun their new life as an independent club, without the Leyton Orient brand name as ballast, they had no home, and Wadham Lodge had given them a place where they could compete. Indeed, they had thrived on the pitch, but renewing a rolling contract every few months was not a viable way to run a football club. With the rising cost of living and increased energy bills, Seaward's latest contracts had brought in an additional hourly charge every time the floodlights were turned on, meaning an even bigger financial outlay.

'We don't want to leave Walthamstow. We are east London kids. We don't want to go that bit further into east London, but we don't have a choice. It seems to be that as with a lot of women's clubs now, we either have to have someone else's name in order to access the facilities and infrastructure or we don't get to play.'

That was not to say that Seaward did not think a close working relationship with men's clubs, even those higher up the footballing pyramid, was possible or useful.

'If you support lower-league men's football in the UK, you should be out there supporting independent women's football clubs as well, because that's where the bleed-over has to be,' said Edwards. 'We would love to have that bleed-over with lower-league men's clubs, I know other independent clubs would, but the barrier is always, "We will do it, but you have to take our name."

'When cities twin, when you see "Stevenage twinned with Shymkent" – there's a sign I've gone past on the motorway enough that I can know it – it doesn't say, "Stevenage twinned with Stevenage (Shymkent, Azerbaijan)". These identities can be separate and complement each other. But our independence is critical to us because if we're not independent, we can't build our own brand and our own identity, we have no USP and we have nothing we can sell.'

Taking the name of a men's club would never be an option for Seaward. It meant that they could have control over things as basic as kit design; if the move to Redbridge panned out as hoped, Seaward would be playing in the same ground as the ex-Ford Motors works team in the year that marked the 55th anniversary of the women's strike at the Dagenham plant, which ultimately led to legislation for equal pay. They were already intending to create a home kit that paid tribute to the courage and achievements of those women, and Edwards pointed out that they would not have been able to if they had been officially linked with a men's team, whose officials would have insisted that the women wear the same kit as the men.

However, it was understandable that many other women's teams were very happy to work within those parameters for the benefits it could bring. Coming under the umbrella of a well-known men's club would increase their profile but would also likely increase their financial coffers; Edwards knew that one team currently playing in the women's tier five had a budget substantially into the seven-figure mark. As a general policy, though, he had concerns towards men's clubs simply being encouraged to adopt a women's team for the publicity and kudos.

'It's a quick fix, and from the perspective of the men's clubs, I can totally understand it: if they are investing a lot into women's football, they want brand value out of it. That is the baseline economics of it, and it's about brand value. If in 20 years' time the women's game starts making money properly, brilliant, but right now it's brand value extension. It's more kits to sell. It's more things to get on to. It's more advertiser space.'

Edwards had developed Seaward's own sponsorship and advertising offering so that big businesses with large budgets for corporate social responsibility projects could invest as well as smaller companies seeking greater exposure and looking to partner with a football club that shared their values. He felt that grassroots clubs such as Seaward were able to be more nimble and responsive with this kind of work in the community, but had been disappointed that even in the wake of England's win in the Euros the previous summer, the emphasis had remained on attracting fans to the elite women's game and supporting their local Women's Super League side rather than their local side full stop.

'Would you say if England's men won the Euros, "This is exactly why you need to go watch your local Premier League team. That's what will help grassroots football"? No one would be saying that. The current women's set-up is sleepwalking into a situation where they become an extension of the men's set-up by default, rather than us preserving our own independent identity. I do think maybe we're raging against the dying of the light.

'But we like raging and we're good at raging, so we're not going to stop doing it.'

12

Change

YASMINE ELGABRY was regretfully considering her future in recreational football. Though she had loved her first full season with Manchester Laces – switching between her usual position as goalkeeper to central midfield in an effort to get more involved – she had recently been promoted at work, stepping up to a more senior and more time-consuming role in politics. Committing to regular Thursday night training seemed an increasingly unlikely challenge when so many political votes and events happened on the same evening.

'I don't think football and politics and my career in general mix,' she said. 'That's part of the reason it's so important for me to play, though, getting to meet people outside of this little political bubble that I can be in – meeting people, experiencing things, doing things. It's part of self-care and supporting my own mental health and wellbeing, and physical wellbeing, of course, and socialising, and the structure – all that is really good for me, and for a lot of people. It's really challenging, though, when I don't always have traditional hours in some ways, like weekends, evenings campaigning, or other projects that come along.'

Her new job meant much more travelling and time spent in London, and it had made her think about how football could and should be kept accessible for people who were also working full-time. Evening fixtures with a 6pm kick-off time were, she pointed out, prohibitive if you had set working hours and were unable to leave early. She was also concerned about the distance of some games in a supposedly local league, meaning hours spent on the road if public transport was not an option. Regardless, she did not want to consider the possibility of moving to another club; Laces trained three minutes from her house, and she felt at home there. She knew other clubs in the area bolstered their lower-ability teams with stronger players, resulting in uncompetitive matches and an unbalanced league, and she did not want to be part of that; she also wanted to be part of a club that aligned with her personal values of inclusivity, particularly in regards to trans players.

Although her time as a regular player might be drawing to a close, Elgabry was grateful for a fine season, and pleased that she would still be able to play with Laces on a Monday night with their drop-in sessions.

'Our second league game of the season, I played in goal, and this [opposing] team was well above the [league] level they were in – we were getting absolutely battered,' she recalled, 'but I played such an amazing game in goal, I've never played in goal like that ever, and I haven't since, to be quite honest. At the end, I was voted player of the match, which was really, really nice, especially because I came out properly bruised – I had a bruise across my chest because someone ran into me. It was really nice just to know the team saw how hard it was as a keeper. It was a hard game, and it was just nice to have that acknowledged.'

After suffering such serious knee problems so early in her life, Elgabry had recovered her confidence on the pitch, reinforced by her more recent switch to the middle of the park.

'I was going in goal and then I wasn't doing anything – what you do as a keeper is pretty minimal usually. Even if your team's only half good, you're not doing much. I was like, "I'm coming to football, I want to get some exercise and I want to move around, and I'm just not getting that."

'So I got to move positions a bit and it's been really good. I've really been enjoying it, and I've definitely noticed a difference in my physical ability because of that, the running and the keeping up with people. My knees have been fine. I've managed to get a billion other injuries, but my knees have been fine, luckily!'

Her most recent knock had been a hamstring tear, incurred when she overstretched and then caught her foot in the ground; having had that knee ligament injury in her younger years, she was well aware it could have been much worse. Still, the hamstring tear was painful.

'It was the first time I've ever cried on the pitch, actually. Even after I tore my ACL, I didn't cry. So that is a bit embarrassing – for no reason, no one else cared!' she said. 'I just couldn't believe it happened. It's such a silly injury because I shouldn't have reached out with my leg the way I did. I should have dived but it happened;

sometimes shots come at you and you don't really expect them to happen.'

Even with her newly acquired experience in midfield, Elgabry still saw herself as fundamentally a goalkeeper, which she felt improved her game.

'I think mentally I'm a keeper in a lot of ways: the way I see the pitch, if I'm able to take shots the way I shoot is the way that I would struggle to get the ball. So it is really interesting. I've always been a keeper that's good with my feet.'

Regardless of what happened with her job and with her football, she thought her experiences across the course of the season were instructive, and highlighted issues that many women were likely to face. She had a career she loved and wanted to give her best to, as well as wanting to spend time with her husband and her friends, plus some time alone to decompress. Football – even at local level – impinged a lot on any spare time.

'Sometimes it's really hard to manage all of these things. I don't know if everyone would be willing to admit that. I think some people are like, "No, football is all I need!" but I definitely feel the need for the other aspects of my life to do well and make sure I don't lose friends or family or whatever between work and football.

'It's not always an easy feat to be available. It's a challenge and I think it's something that, especially as women, you are expected to wear so many hats and do so many things – how do you manage priorities? Like I said, football is a really important part of self-care for me, but you have these other important parts too. What's a priority? I'm not going to lie, sometimes for me, the priority is "it's a team sport and I can't let the team down", and also I pay for it and I need to get my money's worth! Maybe that's not the attitude to have, but sometimes that's the thing that keeps me not avoiding a week so I can be by myself or spend time with my husband.'

* * *

With a handful of games to go, Shrewsbury Town were comfortably still sitting third in the table of the West Midlands Regional Women's Football League Premier Division. They had a game in hand over leaders Sutton Coldfield, who were eight points clear of second-placed Kidderminster Harriers. Shrews were enjoying an unbeaten run in all competitions that stretched back over two months, and included a thumping 8-0 league win over Crusaders.

Captain Vikki Owen had contributed one of the goals, taking her overall tally for the season to four – something she did not tend to expect playing at centre-half.

'I'm doing OK!' laughed Owen. 'We've got quite a few in the team that score goals so we're not relying on one person. One of the girls got a hat-trick at the weekend, and it's nice to be able to share that across the team.'

Maddie Jones was also on the scoresheet against Crusaders. With all cup competitions included, she had surpassed the 30-goal mark for the season a few weeks prior.

'It took a little while to build her up and now she's just unstoppable,' said her captain. 'She's incredible. Her finishing is just unbelievable. She's so small and tiny, but she's so fast, and she always finds a way, which is amazing.'

By this point, at the end of April, Shrewsbury Town had accepted that they would not be promoted this season, but Owen took a great deal of heart from her team's displays and results in their first campaign at this level. She felt that it would stand them in very good stead for next year.

'A couple of slip-ups in games that we probably shouldn't have slipped up in have taken us away from that promotion again, which we potentially could have got,' she said, 'but yeah, we are still doing really well, still really proud.'

She also hoped that the team's success would attract more sponsors, meaning more money to expand in the future, and more players, possibly even drawing them in from a higher level to join a solid Shrewsbury set-up, and she was confident that once a player took part in a training session they would want to stay.

'We are such a nice team, really, I don't think anybody's ever come to a training session and been on their own or felt uncomfortable. They will come and they'll say, "Oh, you are all so welcoming," and that's the kind of vibe we want because we know it can be very cliquey within women's football. Once they've got a starting eleven, it's very hard to come – especially as a female on their own – into a team full of females and go, "I want to try and compete against you." It's a very difficult vibe, actually. I think we're doing well with it at Shrewsbury.'

Montgomery Waters Meadow had been Shrewsbury Town's home for just over a decade and a half following their move from the lovely Gay Meadow, right on the banks of the River Severn. The main stadium had a capacity of nearly 10,000, but the club's foundation and the women's team played on the complex's 3G pitch. There was no seating or covered stands, but a railed area opposite the dugouts so that spectators could lean on the pitchside barrier throughout the match.

It was a lengthy but lovely walk from the town centre, with the residential streets lined with pretty cottages, arts-and-crafts houses, and fascinating passageways leading to small shops and studios. The new stadium was on the outskirts of the town, like so many other grounds designed and constructed at the turn of the millennium, with a nearby retail park packed with megastores, and a huge discount supermarket on the adjacent plot.

It was a drizzly, overcast Sunday afternoon as Shrewsbury Town prepared for their West Midlands League Cup semi-final; coincidentally, it was against Crusaders, the same opposition they had beaten so thoroughly the weekend before. The visitors had arrived in good time, travelling from Birmingham in a coach along with plenty of noisy support.

Shrews manager Tom Peevor had the responsibility of sorting the pitch out before the teams could warm up, ensuring the corner flags were in place, and pushing the portable goals – used for five-a-side and drills – as far back as possible. After greeting the match officials, he was then able to concentrate on getting his side prepared for an important game.

The teams emerged from the dressing rooms located in the cabins next to the pitch, which also housed the public toilets. Though many people would associate Sunday football with the smell of wet grass and mud, the overriding smell here was of the damp rubber on the 3G and the warming ointment laden on the players' legs. As the players walked out, the space on the sidelines began to fill with a flurry of spectators, who had opted to stay sheltered in their cars right to the very last moment.

Right from kick-off, Shrewsbury were dominant. Their sweet passing game suited the surface well, although as the rain grew more intense, the sliding tackles began to disrupt play more, particularly as players landed awkwardly and required treatment. One of the Crusaders players needed lengthy attention on the pitch during the first half, and after having her knee strapped up, was helped over the fence and into the changing rooms.

'I heard a pop,' she told one of her companions, clearly suggesting that she was worried she had incurred an anterior cruciate ligament injury.

Goals from Leanne Rimmer and Zoe Child had the Shrews ahead at the break. Rimmer's years of experience in the women's game were evident, along with her defensive colleague Brogan Cook; both were vocal in their encouragement for the team's younger players, with teenagers Anna France and Lucia Rooney in particular evidently blossoming with the boost in confidence they received from their senior team-mates. It was Rooney – a defender turned attacker – who added the third and final goal of the afternoon, one that she deserved for her hard work, and to a woman her team-mates ran to her to celebrate her achievement.

Captain Vikki Owen was not on the scoresheet, having had three great goalscoring chances but not managing to connect properly with any of them. She, Rimmer and Cook left the pitch laughing in mock disbelief about her failure to score, and commiserating about the toll that the extended periods of injury time had taken on their bodies as they tried to keep warm and keep moving in the chill rain. Reaching a cup final made up for the aches and pains; indeed, it would be their second cup final of the season, having reached the County Cup Final already. That would be in Telford on a Friday evening, a piece of scheduling that bewildered Peevor.

'We never play Fridays!' he pointed out. The League Cup Final was set to take place after the end of the regular season, scheduled for Evesham, a two-hour drive away. He was slightly concerned about how such kick-off days and times might impact his squad, wondering if the governing bodies took into account that players may have to take annual leave from work just to make a Friday evening kick-off. The need for squad depth was one of the reasons he had employed so much rotation throughout the team, using his capacity of substitutes, even switching out his goalkeeper towards the end of the game. This way, the senior players got a little protection as they had already accumulated so many minutes across so many competitions and the younger players got the first-team experience they needed in order to improve and to ensure they were able to step in to the starting eleven if required.

Peevor was, of course, well aware of how his veteran players worked with the younger ones, and was very grateful for it.

'It makes my job so much easier! They're brilliant.'

He laughed. 'They call themselves "the mums"! But they're mentors, really.'

208

* * *

There was one notable absentee from the Shrewsbury side – top goalscorer Maddie Jones, who had gone off with an injury the previous weekend. In the same week as England captain Leah Williamson confirmed that she would miss the forthcoming Women's World Cup with an anterior cruciate ligament injury – just like her Arsenal team-mate Beth Mead – Jones had suffered the same blow.

At the time, she had not realised what she had done. Evading a tackle, she jumped over the oncoming opponent, and landed on her right leg, with her knee buckling. She thought she might have initially dislocated it, and the pain began to ease after treatment from the club physio. Then she went to see a knee specialist – a family friend who squeezed her in at short notice.

'It's your ACL.'

'I was like, "What?" That hadn't even crossed my mind. I don't know why it didn't, the amount of injuries on ACLs at the minute in female football, [but] it did not cross my mind at all.'

Jones was taking the opportunity to find out a bit more about ACL injuries as a whole, circulating a short survey on social media to gather information from male and female footballers who had experience of the problem. She was fascinated to see the number of established risk factors that kept coming up time and again in responses: a particular stage in the menstrual cycle, pitch conditions, footwear, and more.

She was walking with ease, and her short stature meant she was comfortable driving, with her seat close to the steering wheel and her knee thus at a comfortable angle, but she was struggling with bending, stretching, and climbing stairs.

'I feel a bit silly really,' she admitted. 'I'm just walking around as normal as if it's fine, and it's not.

'Now that it's eased, I keep saying to people: I always presumed my ACL would completely have impacted my day-to-day life. I thought it would have been a lot worse than it actually is. I feel like I should be able to do other things, but I can't. I'm walking [but] I just want to get back playing football, but obviously I can't, so it's quite frustrating.'

Of course, as a PE teacher, she was having to take care and stop herself from stretching too far if she was demonstrating a skill; the week after the injury, she jarred the knee again as she showed her students how to catch a ball in a rounders match. She was a permanent fixture on the sidelines of every Shrewsbury match, but she was not a good spectator, however much she was cheering on her team-mates; she found it particularly difficult to watch them knowing that they would be playing in two cup finals without her.

She had seen the former Arsenal and England striker Kelly Smith talk about her own conflicting feelings when she was out through injury, wanting her team to win but also wanting them to notice she wasn't playing, and completely understood what she meant.

'You do want them to miss you. You don't want them to forget about you, [but] if I'm not going to be playing in pre-season next season, they're going to have to recruit some players to fill my position.

'It's hard. I don't want to say they rely on me, because they don't; so many people score within our team, [but] obviously the amount of goals that I've scored, I have contributed to a lot of the goals this season.'

As her team-mates looked ahead to the Friday night final of the Shropshire County Cup, Jones was awaiting the results of the MRI on her knee to reveal the extent of the damage. She had spent part of her bank holiday in hospital having the scan, but had to wait for the consultant's verdict a few days later. While the rest of the squad celebrated winning the cup with a 2-1 victory against Shifnal Town, their joy was tempered with the news that Jones received the morning after: confirmation of an ACL tear and the need for surgery that would keep her out of the majority – if not all – of the 2023/24 season. Unsurprisingly tearful at the news, Jones was staying as positive as she could, buoyed by Shrewsbury's second cup triumph – this time on penalties against Worcester City Women to win the West Midlands Women's League Premier Cup – and focusing on her recovery that she was refusing to rush.

'It's going to be a long journey but I'll do everything I can to make sure I'm back as quickly but safely as I can,' she said.

* * *

Oxford United went into the final Sunday of the league season on top of the FA Women's National League Southern Premier Division. With 21 matches played, they had 16 wins to their credit, three draws and two losses, equalling 51 points on the board. They travelled to third-placed Ipswich Town, who had the same number of wins, one fewer draw, and one more loss, leaving them on 50 points. Sandwiched between them were Watford, who had an identical record to Ipswich but had a better goal difference.

They had already picked up some silverware, winning the Oxfordshire FA County Women's Cup with a thumping 15-0 win against East Oxford Ladies in the final. If Oxford beat Ipswich, they would also win the title, no matter what Watford did in their match against Billericay Town. A draw would also be enough for United – as long as Watford did not win.

Oxford lost. Ipswich's Freya Godfrey scored in the 59th minute – the only goal of the game. To add salt to the wound, Watford enjoyed a thumping 3-0 triumph, securing them the championship and then promotion in the National League play-off final two weeks later. Liam Gilbert's side finished in third.

'We did everything right,' reflected Shelly Provan two days later. 'We did everything Liam wanted us to do in the game tactically. That's football, isn't it? Sometimes on the day it just doesn't happen and that's how it worked out on Sunday, unfortunately.'

She remembered a conversation she had had with Gilbert earlier in the season, back in February when they had lost 2-1 to Cheltenham Town, firmly in mid-table, and he had noticed that she was even more disappointed than the rest of the team.

'He said, "What's wrong?" and I just said, "You can't lose these games." You can't lose these points, and it doesn't matter what time of the season it is, these points are important throughout the season.

'I said, "These are the points that could be the reason we win the league or we don't." Ultimately that is what it comes down to. There's no room for error in this league anymore.'

Nevertheless, Provan described it as one of the best seasons she had ever had. She was full of praise for the squad and the backroom staff as well as for Gilbert's coaching and management.

'To have somebody want you to start every game of the season is incredible for a player, and you can only ever play your best football when you feel like that. We were all saying after the game we have enjoyed being a part of the squad and being a part of the club, and I just hope that the group stays together.'

Provan was about to turn 39. One year ago, she had been considering hanging up her boots, but hated the thought of having the decision forced on her. Now she felt she had proven that she could still play at a high level and on the big occasions, and was trying not to think about retirement and instead opting to 'go with the flow', as she laughingly put it.

'If I did make that decision,' she said thoughtfully, 'I feel like I would have ended on a really nice and enjoyable season. It would have been nicer if we'd won the league, but I feel a bit better about finishing on a high. We'll see.'

Whatever happened, she knew that the whole squad would remember 2022/23 fondly.

'No matter what,' she said, 'we achieved something together that was pretty incredible this year.'

EPILOGUE

WITHIN SIX weeks of England winning the 2022 Women's Euros, colleagues began to talk about the prospects of Gareth Southgate's team winning the men's World Cup in Qatar, and finally 'bringing football home'.

Plenty of these people had happily gone to Wembley for the final in the summer, and they had interviewed some of the team's leading lights. It wasn't that they didn't know what England's women had done; it was that they didn't think it counted, somehow. Or perhaps if it counted, it didn't count quite as much as a victory for the men would.

Since 1966, England's men have reached one major international final – the Euros in 2021. So far, the women have reached three European finals (winning one) and picked up the bronze medal at one Women's World Cup, in 2015. As we see so often, women are required to excel before they get even a modicum of the respect that their male counterparts get just for existing.

But since the Lionesses' glorious victory in the sunny summer of 2022, it has become evident that things have started to change. The casual appearances of England stars on primetime television spoke volumes; Leah Williamson on *The Graham Norton Show*, Millie Bright on *8 out of 10*

Cats – the audience knew who these women were and they were greeted with delight.

Crucially, the Lionesses of the past have also been getting the public recognition they have long deserved, not just from the institutions that had neglected them previously, but from the wider public. When Kerry Davis was inducted into the National Football Museum's Hall of Fame, special guests in the packed audience included Chris Lockwood, of the 1971 unofficial squad that travelled to Mexico, original Lioness Sue Whyatt, and Pat Gregory, founding member of the Women's FA.

There was a panel discussion, in which I had been invited to participate, hosted by Manchester City matchday presenter Harriet Muckle, and in which I was joined by Davis herself as well as journalist Miriam Walker-Khan. In the second half of the evening, we got the chance to ask Davis some questions before throwing it open to the audience. It was strange and thrilling to see so many people there to celebrate one of the long-overlooked stars of English women's football, and to hear what they wanted to say to her and learn about her.

I had also noticed writers and researchers starting to put together historical narratives about some other former players, notably Sylvia Gore, the woman who scored England's first official goal in that match against Scotland in 1972. After her death in the autumn of 2016, I was pleased to play the tiniest of roles to ensure her treasure trove of memorabilia was preserved and also accessible to future historians, helping her next of kin arrange to set up an archive in her name at a university in the north-west.

Knowing how much Sylvia had revelled in her position as ambassador at Manchester City, and how much she loved being part of a club that offered top-class facilities for female professional footballers, I thought of her often in 2022, wishing she had been around to enjoy the year with the rest of her team-mates. It was some consolation to know, though, that members of her family had been invited to all the events celebrating the history of the Lionesses, and that she was remembered and represented.

* * *

'I got a sponsored car, and I used to get my petrol paid for me,' recalled Karen Farley, reflecting on her time playing on the continent during the 1990s. 'But we never had money in our pocket. Just as I finished playing in Sweden, that's when players started getting incentives to go to different teams. And that's when everything started to change.'

The steady flow of money into women's football in England had certainly changed it completely. At the turn of the millennium, the top flight of domestic competition was amateur; its full professionalisation, giving the players the chance to train and play every day, was no small contributory part to the 2022 Euros triumph. Success attracts more money; brands now are battling to sponsor top clubs and sign up leading players as ambassadors. Fans are also snapping up tickets and making it plain that women's football cannot be contained within the small non-league grounds for much longer; Arsenal's Women's Champions League semi-final second leg against Wolfsburg sold out the Emirates Stadium, a far cry from their usual Meadow

Park home with a capacity of under 5,000. If that financial investment trickles downwards to grassroots, supporting the talent pathway for young players but also providing space for women who want to play as a hobby, so much the better.

Plenty of people with years of experience in the women's game, while delighted with the progress they had seen and the rewards the England team were now getting, could not help but sound a slightly cautionary note.

'These young players that are coming up now, they're not going to know any different,' said Farley. 'If they're going to think about the old days, they'd be like, "Well, that doesn't even affect me. That was 30 years ago. I wasn't even born then."

'Money can make things wonderful. That's what they've done to the women's game because it's about money. It's about investment, it's about belief and giving these girls the opportunity and that takes money, at the end of the day. That's what it boils down to, and it succeeded. So hopefully that will continue.

'But the minute you start putting money in people's pockets, it changes something in people's minds and in their hearts.

'"If I go to that team, I'm going to get that." "I'm going there, because I'll get that!" I don't blame people for it. But I hope we're going to have a good few years – quite a lot of years, I'd like to think, of just enjoying it, of just being positive, of there not being any negatives coming out of it, because at the moment there's nothing negative that has come out of the FA's investment and the sponsors' investment and the media's investment, it is all positive.'

One of the FA's developments for the women's and girls' player pathway had been the replacement of the previous 28 regional talent centres and ten advanced coaching centres with up to 70 emerging talent centres for players aged between eight and 16 with elite potential. It followed long-standing concerns about the apparent lack of diversity at the very top level in England, in the Lionesses squad, particularly the lack of racial and ethnic diversity, but also in terms of socio-economic background; with more players able to access more top-level coaching, the intent was that the talent pool would broaden and be more inclusive. The target was to ensure that 95 per cent of players would be able to travel to an emerging talent centre within one hour's journey time of their home by 2024, and to have 4,200 girls on the FA talent programme by the same point, rising from 1,722 in February 2023 when the revamp had been announced. The clubs in the Women's Super League and the Championship were to have professional game academies attached to them, with 20 launching for the 2023/24 season.

Nevertheless, there were already concerns from grassroots players and coaches, worried that the focus on the elite player pathway would mean that those who wanted to play for fun or who were not of high ability would be struggling to find a club to join. For all the excitement and investment at the top level, there were still problems even a few leagues further down. On the last day of their season, tier five Colney Heath Ladies marked their final match affiliated with the men's club of the same name by having to move to a park pitch to play Bowers & Pitsea Ladies; the club's main ground was being used for a bank holiday celebration to commemorate King Charles III's coronation, with a bouncy castle on the pitch.

Finding a place to call home was challenging for many teams. It was a matter of huge relief to Jo Butler-Williams that she had signed the documentation that meant that London Seaward would have a new long-term home at Redbridge for the next ten years. The announcement was made on the same day that Seaward won their first trophy in their new name – the Combined Counties League Women's Cup.

'We're really excited to get it over the line, it's been a long time coming,' she said. The ten-year lease meant that they would be able to access funding but also add touches to the stadium that would make it feel like home: an honours board, for example. The next challenges would be to build links with the community and bring in more fans to establish a consistent income stream, and to create a talent pathway that meant that girls and women of all standards could find a place to play with Seaward. Of course, moving up the league pyramid was also an ambition, but equally important was speaking out – on issues such as the importance of a secure home for women's teams.

'Continuing to be a voice for women's football is such a huge part of what we can do as a women's football club,' she said. 'We are in a unique position, we can be that voice for the game and we are going to continue to do that.'

Helen Hardy was always searching for suitable venues to allow her expanding breadth of Manchester Laces teams to train, and to open up the grassroots game to more and more women and non-binary people. She felt that despite the glamour and success of the elite end of the game, there was still a wariness and mistrust that an amateur club could pull in the required numbers and make it worth a facility's while to give them the space. She also had the ongoing problem of what the footballing set-up still called in shorthand 'legacy bookings' – men's clubs who had been training and playing at a pitch for years, meaning that bigger and busier women's clubs could not get a look-in. That was even the case at Hough End, a new project in Manchester converting playing fields into a full sporting space, complete with stadium and 3G pitches. Hardy had privately hoped to be able to get an area there for Laces, but even prior to construction starting she was told that there was limited space for women's and girls' teams because of the 'legacy bookings'.

'It's like they underestimate us,' she said. 'I don't think they realise that if I got Hough End, every hour of every day, I'd fill it with women. That's unbelievable to them. I can prove it, I can evidence it: evidence it with my business, evidence it with Manchester Laces. I keep evidencing, people will continue to be shocked.'

Hardy wondered if governing bodies across the country needed to step in and create policy to ensure women and girls were getting equal access to facilities, regardless of who had been there first. Manchester Laces' sister team in south London had benefited from the introduction of a new rule where during key time slots – for example, a Tuesday evening between 7pm and 9pm – the space had to be either empty or used for a women's team. Beforehand, clubs had been considering closing because they simply could not get the space to work in. Now, they were expanding even further.

'This policy came in, and within 24 hours, they get a call: "We need you." Firstly, they feel wanted. Secondly, the venue needs them. Thirdly, they're being capped on how much they can charge, so it's like, "We need you and here's a really good price for an 11-a-side pitch for two hours in a prime slot, off you go!"

'They've seen an absolute boom in numbers. That's the power. You give us the room, we will fill it. That's where we're at now with women's football.'

ACKNOWLEDGEMENTS

Thank you so much to the wonderful people from the world of women's football who have allowed me into their lives this season – it's been a pleasure. Thanks to all at Lewes FC Women, London Seaward, Oxford United Women, Shrewsbury Town Women and Manchester Laces, and especially Christine Dunning, Curt Frye, Dan McKimm, Danni Griffiths, Gareth Edwards, Gemma Sims, Giorgia Bracelli, Helen Hardy, Janet Clark née Bagguley, Jamie Edwards, Jenna Legg, Jo Butler-Williams, Jo McDonald, Karen Farley, Kate Chesser, Lauren Heria, Liam Gilbert, Maddie Jones, Maggie Murphy, Natalie Haigh, Sapphire Brewer-Marchant, Shelly Provan, Stef McLoughlin, Sue Whyatt, Tom Peevor, Vikki Owen, Willa Bailey, Yasmine Elgabry, Zahmena Malik and Zoe Taylor.

Thank you to all at Pitch for inviting me to write the third book in the 'Lionesses' series.

Thank you to my literary agent Melanie Michael-Greer for the endless wisdom and support.

And as always, my love and gratitude to my little family: Spring the lurcher, who can be heard in so many Zoom calls, and my husband Julian.

REFERENCES

Batte, Kathryn, 'Arsenal and England star Lotte Wubben-Moy to boycott watching World Cup because the Lionesses' values are "not reflected" in Qatar' (https://www.dailymail.co.uk/sport/football/article-11400795/Arsenal-England-star-Lotte-Wubben-Moy-boycott-watching-World-Cup-Qatar.html)

BBC.co.uk, 'Oxford United Women to bid for WSL2 licence for 2018/19 season' (https://www.bbc.co.uk/sport/football/42973780)

BBC.co.uk, 'Ellen White suffered punctured lung during acupuncture' (https://www.bbc.co.uk/sport/football/62692632)

Collings, Simon, 'The World Cup in Qatar is a tragedy…I won't be watching as normal' (https://www.standard.co.uk/sport/football/leah-williamson-england-world-cup-2022-qatar-lionesses-lgbtq-exclusive-interview-b1042331.html)

FA, 'Finding a new generation through revamped women's and girls' player pathway' (https://www.thefa.com/news/2023/feb/09/womens-player-pathway-revamped-20230902)

Harris, Rob, 'FIFA writes to teams and says focus on the football…not ideological or political battle that exists' (https://www.skysports.com/football/

news/11095/12737790/qatar-world-cup-fifa-writes-to-teams-and-says-focus-on-the-football-not-ideological-or-political-battle-that-exists)

Holbrook, Emma, 'Eidevall: WSL record attendances are sustainable' (https://www.arsenal.com/news/eidevall-wsl-record-attendances-are-sustainable)

Mashiter, Nick, 'Ex-England star Kerry Davis proud to have paved way for generation of success' (https://www.independent.co.uk/sport/football/hall-of-fame-england-national-football-museum-italy-germany-b2222993.html)

Oxford United statement, 6 December 2017 (https://www.oufc.co.uk/news/2017/december/wsl-statement/)

Oxford United statement, 28 May 2018 (https://www.oufc.co.uk/news/2018/may/oxford-united-women/)

Scott, Jill, 'Farewell, Footy' (https://www.theplayerstribune.com/posts/jill-scott-england-soccer-retirement)

Sessions, George, 'Premier League in active conversations with FA about helping women's football' (https://www.independent.co.uk/sport/football/premier-league-richard-masters-wsl-ian-wright-germany-b2136020.html)

Twitter.com, @ellsbells89, 22 August 2022 (https://twitter.com/ellsbells89/status/1561728117793751043/photo/2)

Wubben-Moy, Lotte, 'A playground full of Lionesses' (https://www.arsenal.com/news/playground-full-lionesses-lotte-wubben-moy)